Reimagining Instructional Supervision

Previous Titles by Francis M. Duffy

Courage, Passion, and Vision: A Guide to Leading Systemic School Improvement

Dream! Create! Sustain!: Mastering the Art and Science of Transforming School Systems

Moving Upward Together: Creating Strategic Alignment to Sustain Systemic School Improvement

Power, Politics, and Ethics in School Districts: Dynamic Leadership for Systemic Change

Step-Up-To-Excellence: An Innovative Approach to Managing and Rewarding Performance in School Systems

Strategic Communication During Whole-System Change: Advice and Guidance for School District Leaders and PR Specialists

Reimagining Instructional Supervision

Supervising Knowledge Work

Francis M. Duffy

ROWMAN & LITTLEFIELD
Lanham • Boulder • New York • London

Published by Rowman & Littlefield
A wholly owned subsidiary of The Rowman & Littlefield Publishing Group, Inc.
4501 Forbes Boulevard, Suite 200, Lanham, Maryland 20706
www.rowman.com

Unit A, Whitacre Mews, 26-34 Stannary Street, London SE11 4AB

Copyright © 2017 by Francis M. Duffy

All rights reserved. No part of this book may be reproduced in any form or by any electronic or mechanical means, including information storage and retrieval systems, without written permission from the publisher, except by a reviewer who may quote passages in a review.

British Library Cataloguing in Publication Information Available

Library of Congress Cataloging-in-Publication Data Available

ISBN: 978-1-4758-2271-7 (cloth : alk. paper)
ISBN: 978-1-4758-2272-4 (pbk. : alk. paper)
ISBN: 978-1-4758-2273-1 (electronic)

♾™ The paper used in this publication meets the minimum requirements of American National Standard for Information Sciences—Permanence of Paper for Printed Library Materials, ANSI/NISO Z39.48-1992.

Printed in the United States of America

Contents

Preface   vii

SECTION 1: REIMAGINING INSTRUCTIONAL SUPERVISION   1

1. Instructional Supervision Reimagined   3
2. Core Concepts, Principles, and Tools Underpinning Knowledge Work Supervision   31

SECTION 2: KNOWLEDGE WORK SUPERVISION PROTOCOL   57

3. The Key Players and Their Roles: Creating and Using the Power of Teams   59
4. Step 1: Pre-Launch Preparation   69
5. Step 2: Redesign the Entire System   81
6. Step 3: Create Strategic Alignment   105
7. Step 4: Evaluate Whole-System Transformation   115
8. Step 5: Recycle to Pre-Launch Preparation   127

SECTION 3: PREPARING KNOWLEDGE WORK SUPERVISORS   141

9. Preparing Knowledge Work Supervisors   143
10. Prologue to Revolution   151

Appendices 159
    Appendix A: National Framework of Professional Standards 159
    Appendix B: Proposed Certification Requirements 161

Preface

The history of instructional supervision has been relatively constant. From the days when the first colonists arrived and established schools for their children until today instructional supervision has consistently focused on the critical examination of a teacher's classroom behavior.

In the 1960s, a countermovement in the field of instructional supervision emerged from the work of Morris Cogan, Robert Anderson, and Robert Goldhammer in the Harvard Graduate School of Education; that is, Clinical Supervision. Clinical supervision was more of a coaching model than an evaluation model of supervision and its values were anchored to the belief that teachers are professionals who could benefit from supervisors observing their work and then providing them with feedback. The underlying assumption of both models, I believe, was and still is that teaching and learning can be improved one-teacher-at-a-time through instructional supervision.

Further, if the goal of instructional supervision is to improve teaching and learning then the supervisory process ought to achieve that goal for an entire school system—not just in isolated classrooms or schools within the system. I believe that system-wide instructional improvement cannot and never will happen one-teacher-at-a-time.

The assumption that system-wide instructional improvement can happen one teacher at a time is faulty. There appears to be no convincing evidence that instructional supervision in either form (as teacher evaluation or as clinical supervision) has done much to improve teaching and learning throughout the entire school systems. If traditional supervision cannot improve teaching and learning on a broad scale then the instructional supervision process needs to be re-imagined and transformed (not reformed) to redesign entire school districts into a high-performing knowledge-creating systems.

TRANSFORM AMERICA'S SCHOOL SYSTEMS, NOT REFORM THEM

There is a systemic crisis in American education. It's not new. Many know it. Some deny it. Some are blissfully unaware of it. Some don't want to resolve it because their careers are built around trying to resolve it. Repeated attempts to resolve the crisis have failed and will continue to fail because the approach to resolving the crisis (short-term quick fixes otherwise known as piecemeal change) is outdated and ineffective.

Many of us believe that the crisis is causally linked to the paradigm driving America's education system and its school systems, which is commonly referred to as the Industrial Age paradigm. This paradigm has reached the limit of its performance capacity and there is nothing that can be done to improve its effectiveness in any significant way. Nevertheless, educators, consultants, and policymakers continue to shoot their "silver bullets" at the underperforming and average-performing systems thinking that this time, this one last time, the silver-bullet solutions will work and the systems will significantly improve. Despite their valiant and well-intentioned efforts school systems cannot and will never significantly improve as long as the systems are driven by the old paradigm. The old paradigm has run its course. It ran it well, but now it has reached the end of its usefulness and it must be replaced if we want to ensure that the America's children receive the education they need and deserve.

This crisis in the education system has created a very real "mess" (a term coined by Ackoff (1974) to describe complex, seemingly unsolvable problems) in America's more than 14,000 school systems and failure to transform these school systems to dissolve the "messes" could create a society that is unfit for success and prosperity in the middle to late twenty-first century. The crisis/mess is that our school systems are not designed to educate children for success in our twenty-first-century Knowledge-Age society; that is, there is a huge gap between what and how we teach children during their years in a school system and what and how we could and should be teaching them.

The industrial age paradigm guiding, teaching and learning, and influencing the design and performance of America's school systems is composed of a set of theories, concepts, principles, mental models, and mind-sets. The industrial age paradigm influencing the performance of school systems emerged at the beginning of the Industrial Age in the late 1700s. This paradigm created a factory model for educating groups of students by requiring them to learn a fixed amount of knowledge in a fixed amount of time. That paradigm continues to control the performance of school systems throughout the United States.

There is no place in the controlling paradigm for providing each child with an educational experience that is tailored to his or her needs, interests, and abilities. Because of this significant feature, that paradigm always has and always will leave children behind. Leaving children behind is an unavoidable consequence of the Industrial-Age design of America's school systems. The systems are perfectly designed to get the results they are getting.

REIMAGINING INSTRUCTIONAL SUPERVISION TO TRANSFORM SCHOOL SYSTEMS

I believe that the focus of instructional supervision needs to shift off of individual teachers to focus on transforming the organization design and functioning of entire school systems. Instead of observing teachers working in their classrooms a re-imagined instructional supervision process would focus on redesigning three sets of key system variables:

- *Transform the system's environmental relationships.* Transform the way school systems interact with external stakeholders by moving away from a crisis-oriented, reactive approach to an opportunity-seeking, proactive approach.
- *Transform the system's core and support work.* Transform the way teachers teach and how children learn (the core work) by replacing group-based, teacher-centered instruction with personalized, learner-centered instruction (if a child receives a personalized learning experience that is customized to respond to his or her needs, interests, and abilities and if that child is given the time he or she needs to master the required content, how can that child ever be left behind?) and transform the services that support teaching and learning (the support work).
- *Transform the system's internal social infrastructure.* Transform the quality of work life for teachers, administrators, and support staff by transforming a school system's organization culture, reward system, job descriptions, and so on, to align with the requirements of the new teaching and learning processes (if teachers and staff are demotivated and dissatisfied, they will not use the new teaching and learning paradigm effectively. The quality of work life has a direct and significant impact on motivation and satisfaction).

MAKING THE NEED FOR TRANSFORMATION PERSONAL FOR YOU

Imagine that your school system was seized yesterday by its state department of education and that it was completely shut down. The next day you learn that your district has been given a reprieve, but only if you completely transform the system. You are in charge of the transformation. If you were or are a senior administrator in a school system and if you had the opportunity to transform the way your district relates to its external environment, what changes would you make? Would you create a relationship between your district and its environment that was mutually beneficial? Would you design ways to engage members of your community in constructive conversations about your system's future?

Imagine that you have a large cohort of bright-eyed kindergarten children excited by the prospects of learning, including your child or grandchild. It's your and your colleagues' responsibility to decide how those children will learn and what they will learn over their years in your transformed school system. How would you transform your school system so that it is significantly and substantively different than the one you have now? Would you want teachers to know and understand each child's learning style, academic interests, and intellectual strengths and weaknesses? Would you want each child to be given the time he or she needs to master important knowledge and to satisfy important standards of learning?

If you were or are a teacher and if you had the opportunity to transform the work environment of your school system, what changes would you make? Would you create a more democratic work environment? Would you design ways to stimulate motivation, boost morale, and increase commitment to the overall success of the school system? Would you reshape your school system's reward system to recognize and value high performance?

If you were or are a teacher or administrator and if you had the opportunity to transform the way you and your colleagues create change, how would you ensure that important and meaningful changes are sustained and institutionalized? Would you replace "silver bullet" quick fixes with changes based on principles of whole-system transformational change? Would you figure out creative and effective ways to sustain important and effective changes no matter how often leaders come and go in your system?

WHAT YOU WILL LEARN FROM THIS BOOK

I believe that transformational change can be achieved by using a methodology called Knowledge Work Supervision (KWS)—a reimagined instructional supervision process that focuses on the organization design and performance of entire school systems instead of focusing on the classroom behavior of individual teachers. This methodology is described in great detail in this book.

The book is divided into three sections. Section 1 has two chapters that lay a foundation for the KWS methodology. Chapter 1 offers a rationale for re-imagining instructional supervision. Chapter 2 describes several key concepts, principles, and tools that are part of the KWS methodology.

Section 2 dives deep into the KWS methodology. Chapter three describes KWS key players and their roles. Chapter 4 describes KWS Step 1: Pre-Launch Preparation. Chapter 5 describes Step 2: Redesign the Entire System. Chapter 6 describes Step 3: Create Strategic Alignment. Chapter 7 focuses on Step 4: Evaluate Whole-System Performance. And chapter 8 discusses Step 5: Recycle to Pre-Launch Preparation.

Because KWS requires professionals who can lead complex transformational change it is imperative that state departments of education create a professional license or certificate for Knowledge Work Supervisors and for graduate-level education leadership departments to create new training programs (degree-granting and non-degree) to prepare educators to perform as Knowledge Work Supervisors. Section 3 offers a proposal for creating a change leadership academy to prepare Knowledge Work Supervisors. There are also two appendices that support chapter 9. Finally, chapter 10 brings closure to the book by providing a rationale for a new future for our education system and its component school districts.

I predict that this book and the KWS methodology will be met with skepticism, especially by those whose careers are anchored to traditional supervision and the traditional organization design of school systems. I also predict that there will be visionaries who see the promise of KWS as a methodology to transform entire school systems into high-performing knowledge-creating systems. Those visionaries—the revolutionaries—will meet stiff resistance when advocating for KWS and its vision of transformed school systems. They will be called heretics for proposing changes to traditional supervision. They will be called naïve for suggesting that school districts can and should be transformed. Their ideas set forth in written form or presented at conferences will be sorely criticized as not being research-based, or not being well-written, or not being realistic. And worst of all they and their writings and teachings might be ignored or pushed to the periphery of the profession and labeled as irrelevant.

My message to the visionaries is this: Persist! You will need courage, passion, and vision to keep pushing forward. You will need courage to stand your ground in the face of the adversity that you will encounter as you advocate for KWS. You will need passion to give you the emotional energy you need to keep pushing forward. And you will need to know and understand the vision for transformed school systems that KWS offers. That vision will be your North Star to keep you moving in the right direction. And, you need all three of those traits—courage, passion, and vision. I know courageous people with no vision. I know people with powerful visions but they don't have the guts to stand and fight against their adversaries. They bow down or flee in the face of adversity. And I know people with powerful visions who have courage but who lack the physical and emotional stamina to keep moving forward—the kind of stamina that is driven by the passion to succeed.

I pray that our society will soon find the will and the capacity to transform America's school systems into high-performing knowledge-creating systems driven by the principles of personalized learning. And I offer this book and the KWS methodology as a starting point for developing that will and capacity.

Section 1

REIMAGINING INSTRUCTIONAL SUPERVISION

Section 1 builds a foundation for an innovative approach to instructional supervision—an approach that shifts the focus of supervision off individual teachers and onto a school system's relationship with its external environment, its core and support work processes, and its internal social infrastructure. That innovative approach is called Knowledge Work Supervision (KWS).

Chapter 1 begins by describing the main characteristics of the two dominant approaches to instructional supervision: supervision as evaluation and clinical supervision. A discussion of why those two approaches fail to improve instruction throughout an entire school system is presented. Next, readers are introduced to a brief definition of the term "knowledge work," a term coined by Peter Drucker. Finally, a vision for a new form of instructional supervision is presented—a new approach called "Knowledge Work Supervision".

One of the important goals of KWS is to enhance the professional intellect of teachers. KWS assumes that school systems are knowledge creating organizations and that teachers are knowledge workers. Knowledge organizations create or use knowledge to deliver high quality products or services to customers. Teachers use their professional intellect to organize and deliver information to their students. In chapter two, more details about enhancing teachers' professional intellect to helps them become more effective knowledge workers. Enhancing professional intellect is one of the main goals of transforming a school system's core and support work processes.

Chapter two presents core concepts, principles, and tools that support the KWS methodology. Several key propositions are presented at the beginning of the chapter followed by an in-depth description of the knowledge base informing KWS, including an overview of sociotechnical systems theory, team-based organization design, Future Search, Participative Design Workshops, and Open Space Technology, among others.

Chapter One

Instructional Supervision Reimagined

In spite of all the change activity in the name of school reform, very little has changed in school systems. Longstanding complaints about the performance of school systems still exist. This lack of sustained improvement in teaching and learning may be the result of piecemeal change and the persistence of the Industrial Age paradigm of education. Our school districts need to be perceived as living systems that must be transformed to provide children with an education that is tailored to their individual needs, interests, and abilities and that prepares them for success in our Knowledge-Age society. School systems need to be transformed—not tinkered with—if we are to achieve this vision.

One of the traditional approaches to improving teaching and learning is instructional supervision in either or both of its common forms: supervision as teacher evaluation and clinical supervision. There was, and is, a critically unspoken, but faulty, assumption underlying both forms of traditional supervision; that is, it is assumed that teaching and learning can be improved throughout an entire school or school system one teacher at a time. The one-teacher-at-a-time assumption is not only faulty, but it is also dangerous because it deludes educators into believing that they can improve teaching and learning simply by observing individual teachers and giving them feedback on their teaching performance.

However, those who practice and teach whole-system change have substantial evidence that system-wide improvement does not happen one person at a time; for example, Beer, Eisenstat, and Spector (1990) argued that organizational change does not happen by changing individual behavior. They said that attempts to change organizations are guided by a theory of change that is fundamentally flawed. The common belief is that the place to begin is with the knowledge and attitudes of individuals. Changes in attitudes ... lead to change in individual behavior ... and changes in individual behavior, repeated by many people will result in organizational change ... This theory gets the change process exactly backward. In fact, individual behavior is powerfully shaped by the organizational roles that people play. The most effective way to change behavior, therefore, is to put people into a new organizational context, which imposes new roles, responsibilities, and relationships on them. (p. 159)

The "new organizational context" for school districts is a school system transformed to revolutionize (1) a school system's relationship with its environment, (2) its core and support work processes, and (3) its internal social infrastructure. A new form of instructional supervision is needed to revolutionize teaching and learning throughout an entire school system. That new form of instructional supervision is called Knowledge Work Supervision (KWS) (Duffy, 1995, 1996; Duffy, Rogerson, & Blick, 2000).

KNOWLEDGE WORK AND KNOWLEDGE-CREATING ORGANIZATIONS

KWS assumes that school systems are knowledge-creating organizations and that teachers are *knowledge workers*, a term coined by Peter Drucker (1985, 1993, 1995). Knowledge organizations create or use knowledge to deliver high-quality products or services to customers. Teachers as knowledge workers use their professional intellect to organize and deliver information to their students.

In today's knowledge organizations, there are two types of interrelated work processes: linear work and nonlinear knowledge work. Linear work processes are tightly sequenced and prescriptive (e.g., the traditional instructional program organized as grade levels). Nonlinear knowledge work is the thinking process professionals use to accomplish work tasks. It is "characterized primarily by the creative manipulation of symbols by the mind, whereas so-called routine work is characterized primarily by the creative manipulation of objects by the body" (Christensen, cited in Purser, 1991, p. 3).

The primary tool of knowledge workers is their professional intellect (Quinn, Anderson, & Finkelstein, 1996). Quinn et al. said: "The capacity to manage human intellect—and to convert it into useful products and services—is fast becoming the critical executive skill of the age" (p. 71). Further, these authors said that professional intellect operates at four levels: *cognitive knowledge* (knowing what to do), *advanced skills* (knowing how to do it), *systems understanding* (knowing why it must be done), and *self-motivated creativity* (caring about why it should be done) (p. 72).

Knowledge workers use information to produce new knowledge, design products, or deliver services. The knowledge work process has five components: quality information, key people who participate in an exchange of this information, varied forums for exchanging this information, effective technological devices to support the work, and high-quality work procedures and organizational functions (adapted from Pava, 1983).

Knowledge-creating systems also have an intricate social infrastructure composed of organization design, organization culture, quality of work life, and communication processes, among others. The social infrastructure is inextricably connected to the organization's core and support work processes.

Knowledge-creating systems also exist within a broader environment and the organizations' relationships with the external environment affect the quality and effectiveness of their core and support work processes and their internal social infrastructure.

To increase the effectiveness of knowledge work in school systems, simultaneous change must happen in the three areas identified above: the system's relationship with its external environment, its core and support work processes, and its internal social infrastructure. KWS provides a systemic and systematic model for enhancing and managing knowledge work in school systems.

The challenge of managing knowledge work, however, is that traditional methods for managing knowledge work in school systems do not and cannot work because they are inadequate processes. These traditional methods are instructional supervision and staff development. Traditional supervision is inadequate because it focuses on an examination of the behavior of individual knowledge workers (aka teachers) with the assumption that only if enough individuals improve their individual professional knowledge will the effectiveness of the entire school system improve. Although supervision may help an individual teacher improve, entire school systems are not improved one person at a time.

Traditional staff development is also inadequate because this collection of activities designed for knowledge workers (sometimes by knowledge workers) does not take into account how professionals construct knowledge. These activities provide information, but information is not knowledge and knowledge is not wisdom. Special methods are required that go beyond traditional training to help knowledge workers transform information into knowledge and to develop wisdom in applying that knowledge.

The special methods to transform information into knowledge and then to develop wisdom need to incorporate principles recognizing that professional intellect operates at four levels: cognitive knowledge, advanced skills, systems understanding, and self-motivated creativity (Quinn et al., 1996, p. 72). These methods also need to capitalize on principles of mindful learning

(Langer, 1997, p. 2) which explode seven pervasive myths about learning. These myths are as follows:

- The basics must be learned so well that they become second nature.
- Paying attention means staying focused on one thing at a time.
- Delaying gratification is important.
- Rote memorization is necessary.
- Forgetting is a problem.
- Intelligence is knowing "what's out there."
- There are right and wrong answers.

SUPERVISING KNOWLEDGE WORK

Improving education outcomes in the United States has focused on teaching and learning in individual classrooms and school buildings. This approach is called school-based or site-based improvement and uses traditional instructional supervision (supervision-as-evaluation and clinical supervision). Lewis Rhodes, former Deputy Director of the American Association of School Administrators commented on the deficiencies of this "every school for itself" approach when he said,

> It was a lot easier 30 years ago when John Goodlad popularized the idea of the school building as the fundamental unit of change.... But now it is time to question that assumption—not because it is wrong—but because it is insufficient. Otherwise, how can we answer the question: "If the building is the primary unit at which to focus change efforts, why after 30 years has so little really changed?" (Rhodes, 1997, p. 19)

Rhodes' observations remain true today.

Improving teaching and learning throughout an entire school system requires a new model of instructional supervision that shifts the focus of supervision off individual teachers and schools and focuses instead on the whole school system. This model is called KWS (Duffy, 1995, 1996; Duffy, Rogerson, & Blick, 2000). KWS complies with the observations by Beer et al. quoted above.

KNOWLEDGE WORK SUPERVISION

KWS is a school system transformation model that has the potential to build a school system's capacity to create and sustain meaningful systemic improvements that benefit the children and adults who serve their educational needs, interests, and abilities. KWS is a whole-system transformation methodology especially designed for school districts where faculty and staff reimagine how their school systems can provide children with an education that prepares them for success in our twenty-first-century Knowledge-Age society. Now, let's contrast KWS to traditional approaches to managing change in school systems.

THE TRADITIONAL APPROACH TO MANAGING CHANGE

The three-pronged approach to transformational change described earlier is quite different from the traditional approach to managing change developed by Lewin (1951), which is still taught in some education administration and leadership programs throughout the United States. What Lewin said is that to create change in an organization people first envision a desired future. Then, they assess their current situation and compare the present to the future, looking for gaps between what they have and what they desire.

Next, they develop a transition plan composed of long-range goals and short-term objectives that will move their organization straight forward toward its desired future. Along the way there will be some unanticipated events that emerge, but it is assumed that the "strength" of anticipatory intentions (goals, objectives, strategic plans) will keep those unexpected events under control and thereby keep the system on a relatively straight change-path toward the future. The problem with this approach is that it doesn't work in contemporary organizations.

The complexities of contemporary society, the pressure for rapid change, the increasing number of unanticipated events and unintended consequences during change, and what we know about transforming organizations have created three serpentine change-paths to the future: Path 1—transform a school system's relationships with its environment; Path 2—transform its core and support work processes; and Path 3—transform its internal social infrastructure.

The three-path metaphor is very important because if change-leaders assume that there is a single strategic path from the present to the future that is relatively straight forward when there are actually three winding paths, then as they start transforming their system they will soon be off the true paths and lost. When off course and lost, people and their systems often revert back to their old ways, thereby enacting Jean-Baptiste Alphonse Karr's often quoted French folk wisdom, "The more things change, the more they stay the same" (date unknown).

To move an entire school system along the three paths identified above, change-leaders need a whole-system transformation protocol that will serve as a map to locate and navigate the three nonlinear paths to higher student, teacher and staff, and whole-system learning. Further, this kind of change protocol will only work if certain conditions exist within the school systems and if the protocol is based on key concepts and principles for navigating whole-system change, some of which are identified below with others being explored more comprehensively in chapter 2.

THREE PATHS TO IMPROVEMENT

Over the past half-century a lot has been learned about how to improve entire systems. One of the core principles of whole-system change is that three sets of key organizational variables must be transformed simultaneously (see Pasmore, 1988). These three sets of system variables are characterized as change-paths in the KWS protocol.

Path 1: Transform the District's Relationship With Its External Environment

A school district is an open system. An open system is one that interacts with its environment by exchanging a valued product or service in return for needed resources. If educators want their district to become a high-performing knowledge-creating system, they need to have a positive and supporting relationship with stakeholders in their district's external environment. But they can't wait until they transform their district to start working on these relationships. They need positive and supporting relationships shortly before they begin making important changes within their district. So, they start to transform their district's relationships with key external stakeholders as they prepare their school system to begin its transformation journey.

Path 2: Transform the District's Core and Support Work Processes

Core work is the most important work of any organization. In school districts, the core work is teaching and learning (Duffy, 2003). Core work is maintained and enriched by support work. In school districts, support work roles include administrators, supervisors, education specialists, librarians, cafeteria workers, janitors, bus drivers, and others. Support work is important to the success of a school district, but it is not the most important work. Classroom teaching and learning is the most important work and must be elevated to that status if a school system wants to increase its overall effectiveness. When trying to improve a school system, both the core and support work processes must be transformed.

Further, the entire core work process must be examined and transformed, not just parts of it (e.g., not just the middle school, not just the language arts curriculum, or not just the high school). One of the reasons the entire work process must be transformed is because of a systems improvement principle expressed as "upstream errors flow downstream" (Pasmore, 1988).

Focusing on the entire work process reflects the fact that mistakes made early in a work process flow downstream where they are compounded and create more problems later on in the process; for example, consider a comment made by a high school principal when he first heard a description of this principle. He said, "Yes, I understand. And, I see that happening in our district. Our middle school program is being 'dumbed down' and those students are entering our high school program unprepared for our more rigorous curriculum. And, there is nothing we can do about it." Upstream errors always flow downstream.

Improving student learning is an important goal for transforming core and support work processes of a school district. But focusing only on improving student learning is a piecemeal approach to improvement. A teacher's knowledge and skill are probably two of the most important factors influencing student learning (Learning Point Associates, date unknown). So, taking steps to enhance teachers' professional intellect must also be a part of any school district's improvement efforts to improve student learning.

Improving student and teacher learning is an important goal of improving work in a school district. But this is still a piecemeal approach to improving a school district. A school district is a knowledge-creating system and it is, or should be, a learning organization. Professional knowledge must be created and embedded in a school district's operational structures, and organizational learning must occur if a school district wants to develop and maintain the capacity to provide children with a quality education. So, school system learning (that is, organizational learning) must also be part of a district's transformation strategy to redesign its core and support work processes.

Path 3: Transform the District's Internal Social Infrastructure

Transforming work processes to improve learning for students, teachers and staff, and the whole school system is an important goal, but it is still a piecemeal approach to change. It is possible for a school district to have a fabulous curriculum with extraordinarily effective instructional methods but still have an internal social "infrastructure" (which includes organization culture, organization design, communication patterns, power and political dynamics, reward systems, and so on) that is demotivating, dissatisfying, and demoralizing for teachers. Demotivated, dissatisfied, and demoralized teachers cannot and will not use a fabulous curriculum in remarkable ways.

In addition to transforming how the work of a district is done, transformation efforts must focus simultaneously on redesigning a district's internal social infrastructure because it is important to ensure that the new social infrastructure and the new work processes complement each other. The best way to ensure this complementarity is to make simultaneous improvements to both elements of a school system.

Hopefully, this three-path metaphor makes sense because the principle of simultaneous improvement is absolutely essential for effective whole-system transformation (see Emery, 1977; Pasmore, 1988; Trist, Higgin, Murray & Pollack, 1963). In the literature on systemic change, this principle is called joint optimization (Cummings & Worley, 2001, p. 353).

THE KWS PROTOCOL

KWS is a five-step process that is cyclical. Its structure is illustrated in figure 1.1. The KWS journey proceeds as follows (Section 2 offers more details about the KWS methodology):

- Step 1: Engage in Pre-Launch Preparation.
- Step 2: Transform the Entire System.
- Step 3: Create Strategic Alignment.
- Step 4: Evaluate Whole-System Performance.
- Step 5: Recycle to Pre-Launch Preparation.

Step 1: Pre-Launch Preparation

One of the most common reasons for failed transformation efforts is the lack of good preparation and planning (Kotter, 1996). What happens during the preparation phase will significantly influence the success (or failure) of a district's transformation journey. So, change-leaders have to take the time to do these activities carefully. Quick fixes almost always eventually fail even though they may produce an illusion of improvement.

The early pre-launch preparation activities are conducted by the superintendent of schools and several hand-picked subordinates. At least one member of this small team must be a skillful and highly regarded school public relations specialist. All of these people comprise a "pre-launch team." The superintendent may also wish to include one or two trusted school board members on this small starter team. It is also important to know that this small team is temporary and will not lead the transformation journey that will be

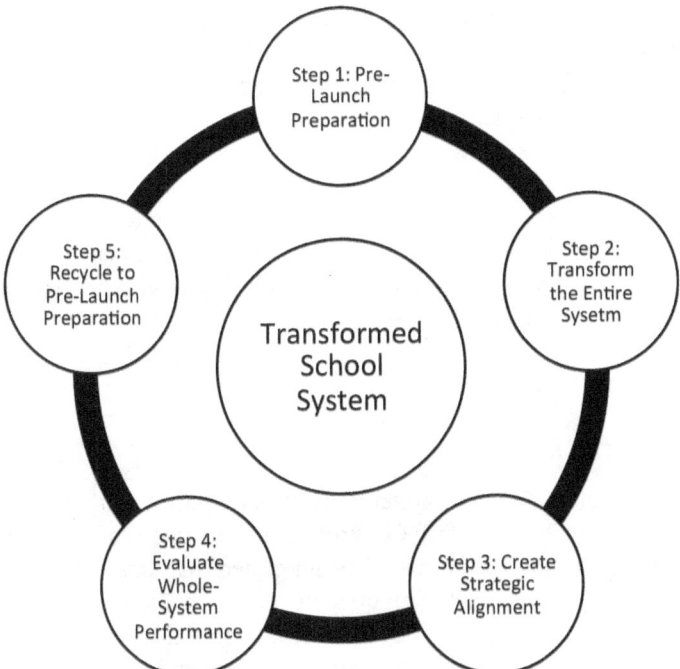

Figure 1.1 **Structure of the Knowledge Work Supervision Steps.**

launched later in the preparation phase. This team only has one purpose—to complete early activities to assess the district's readiness to engage in transformational change.

There are many pre-launch preparation activities (see Duffy 2003, 2004.). They are all important. Some of the tasks should be initiated simultaneously (e.g., building political support among internal and external stakeholders while simultaneously scouting out "best practices" and funding sources to support the change process). Others need to be sequenced as follows:

1. Assess and document the need for the district to change and identify opportunities from which the district could benefit.
2. Develop clear and powerful public relations messages about the needs and opportunities.
3. Organize a Community Engagement Conference.
4. Organize a System Engagement Conference.

Sirkin, Keenan, and Jackson (2005) identified four key factors that affect the success or failure of a transformation effort. These factors should be addressed during the pre-launch preparation phase. Sirkin, Keenan, and Jackson called these the "hard factors of change." They are

- *duration*: the amount of time needed to complete the transformation initiative;
- *integrity*: the ability of the change-leadership teams to complete the transformation activities as planned and on time, which is directly affected by the team members' knowledge and skills for leading a transformation journey;
- *commitment*: the level of unequivocal support for the transformation demonstrated by senior leadership, as well as by employees; and
- *effort*: the amount of effort above and beyond normal work activities that is needed to complete the transformation.

Let's look at each of these factors more closely.

Hard Factor #1: Duration

There is a common assumption that transformation efforts that require longer timelines are more likely to fail. Contrary to this common assumption, Sirkin, Keenan, and Jackson's (2005) research suggested that long-term transformation efforts that are evaluated frequently are more likely to succeed than short-term projects that are not evaluated. It seems that the frequent use of formative evaluation during a transformation journey has a significant positive effect on the success of that journey.

Hard Factor #2: Integrity

The question this factor addresses is, "Can we rely on the change-leadership teams that we create to facilitate the transformation journey?" The importance of the answer to this question cannot be understated. The success of a district's transformation journey will be directly affected by the attitudes, knowledge, and skills of the people who staff the various teams that must be chartered and trained to provide change-leadership. School systems need to get their best people on these teams, where "best" means smart, skilled, articulate, influential, and unequivocally committed to transforming their school system.

Hard Factor #3: Commitment

Transformational change must be led from the top of a school district. The superintendent must not only provide verbal support for the transformation, but he or she must also demonstrate unequivocal behavioral support by participating in transformation activities.

Initial commitment to the transformation journey must also be present among approximately 25 percent of a school system's faculty and staff. This cadre of supporters is called a "critical mass" (Being First, 2006). Block's

Instructional Supervision Reimagined

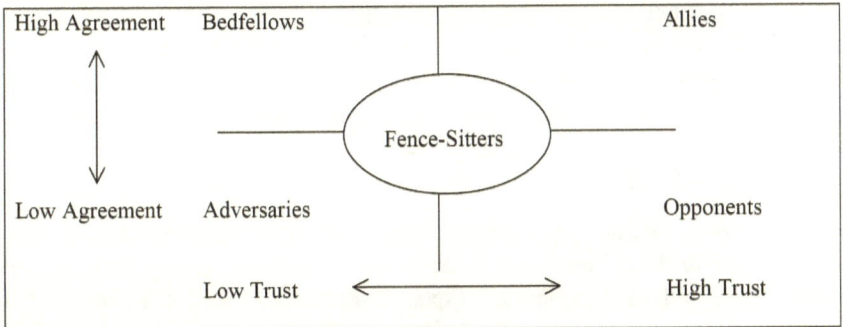

Figure 1.2 Block's Model for Political Groups in Organizations

discussion of political groups in organizations offered an effective way to identify who does and who does not support change in organizations (1986). His model shown in figure 1.2 can be modified to identify whose political support is needed to launch and then sustain a district's transformation journey.

Block used two dimensions (vertical and horizontal) to identify five political groups in organizations. When adapted to support a district's transformation journey, the vertical axis of his model represents the level of agreement (low to high) with a district's transformation goals. The horizontal axis represents the level of trust (low to high) between faculty, staff, and the change-leaders. The intersection of these two axes creates four political groups, with a fifth group straddling the well-known and often lamented "fence":

1. Allies: people who strongly agree with the transformation goals and who are highly trusted;
2. Opponents: people who do not agree with the transformation goals but with whom there is a high degree of trust—it may be possible to convert these people into allies;
3. Bedfellows: people who agree with the transformation goals but who are not highly trusted because they may withdraw their support at a later time;
4. Adversaries: people who disagree with the transformation goals and who are not highly trusted; and
5. Fence-sitters: people who cannot decide where they stand on the goal of transforming their school district. They usually have a wait-and-see attitude toward the changes that are being proposed.

Block offered strategies for communicating with each group. These strategies can be used during the pre-launch preparation phase to build internal political support for a district's transformation journey while remembering that about 25 percent of the system's faculty and staff must support the change effort. This critical mass of supporters will likely be found in the allies and bedfellows groups with the possibility of converting some of the opponents to allies and by moving some of the fence-sitters off the fence and into the allies group. It is unlikely that adversaries can be converted to allies or bedfellows.

Hard Factor #4: Effort

When planning the transformation of a school district, change-leaders sometimes don't realize or don't know how to deal with the fact that faculty and staff are already busy with their day-to-day responsibilities (see Objection #3 later in this chapter). If in addition to these existing responsibilities faculty and staff are asked to join the change-leadership teams that are required to transform their district, their level of resistance toward the transformation journey might increase.

Sirkin, Keenan, and Jackson (2005, p. 6) suggested that ideally the workload of key employees (i.e., those who have direct change–leadership responsibilities) should not increase more than 10 percent during a transformation effort. Beyond the 10-percent limit, the resources for change will be overstretched, employee morale will plummet, and interpersonal and intergroup conflict will increase. Therefore, decisions must be made about how to manage the workload of the people who are invited to join the teams that are formed to lead the KWS journey.

At some point during the pre-launch phase, a decision will be made about the system's readiness to launch a full-scale transformation journey; that is, the pre-launch team will make a "launch/don't launch" decision. If a launch decision is made, then a new leadership team is chartered and trained to provide strategic leadership for the duration of the transformation journey. This team, because of its purpose, is called a Strategic Leadership Team (SLT). It is composed of the superintendent and several others, including teachers and building administrators appointed to the team by their peers (not by the superintendent). This team also appoints and trains a Knowledge Work Supervisor who provides tactical leadership for the KWS journey.

Near the end of the pre-launch preparation phase, the SLT and Knowledge Work Supervisor organize and conduct a one- to three-day Community Engagement Conference that can bring into a single room hundreds of carefully selected people from the community who then self-organize into smaller discussion groups around topics related to the district's transformation effort. This conference is designed using Owen's Open Space Technology design principles (1991, 1993). The results of this conference are used as front-end data for another large group event for the district's faculty and staff that is scheduled early in KWS Step 2. That second event is called a System Engagement Conference.

The System Engagement Conference is a strategic planning conference that brings the whole system into one room. This conference uses the design principles of Weisbord and Janoff's *Future Search*(2010). Bringing the whole system into the room, however, doesn't mean that every single person who works in the school district participates in the conference. Instead, the SLT and Knowledge Work Supervisor ask each department, team, and unit within the district to send at least one person to participate in the conference. In this way, the whole system is represented in the conference room.

The outcome of the System Engagement Conference is a new strategic framework for the district that includes a new mission, a new vision, and a new strategic plan, as well as parameters for guiding the transformation journey. This framework is also informed by data collected from external stakeholders who participated in the earlier Community Engagement Conference.

As stated earlier, the "target system" for KWS is an entire school system rather than individual schools or work units within a system. Although the entire system is the target system, the KWS journey is navigated by organizing the system into academic clusters (groups of schools and programs), a cluster for the central administration, and a cluster for all nonacademic support work units. The academic clusters must include at least one school-based administrator and one teacher from each level of schooling within the cluster (e.g., in a preK–12th grade cluster there should be one administrator and one teacher from the elementary, middle, and secondary levels of schooling). This membership formula ensures that the entire instructional program within an academic cluster is represented.

One cluster is also formed for the central office staff. This cluster includes all the functions housed in the central administration unit. Finally, there is a cluster formed for the nonacademic support work units (e.g., cafeteria, building and grounds maintenance, and transportation).

All of these clusters are formed to facilitate the district's transformation journey. Each cluster has a Cluster Redesign Team that is trained in the principles of whole-system change. Each team guides the KWS transformation journey within its respective cluster. The daily work of all the Cluster Redesign Teams (CRTs) is coordinated by the Knowledge Work Supervisor. The SLT provides broad strategic oversight of the teams and supervises the Knowledge Work Supervisor.

Step 2: Transform the Entire System

Navigating whole-system change requires simultaneous transformations along three paths:

- Path 1: Transform the district's relationship with its external environment (which improves relationships with key external stakeholders).

- Path 2: Transform the district's core and support work processes (core work is teaching and learning; support work includes secretarial work, administrative work, cafeteria work, building maintenance work, and so on).
- Path 3: Transform the district's internal social infrastructure (which includes organization design, governance, policies, organization culture, reward systems, job descriptions, communication, and so on).

Making simultaneous changes along these three paths is a core principle from the field of organization development (see Emery, 1977; Pasmore, 1988; Trist, Higgin, Murray, and Pollack, 1963). This principle is often called joint optimization (Cummings & Worley, 2001).

Prior to engaging faculty and staff in their clusters' transformation journeys, the people invited to participate in the workshops must receive training on principles of systemic change, on the nature of knowledge work, and about the mission and vision of their district. At the completion of the training, each Cluster Redesign Team organizes a Cluster Engagement Conference by using Weisbord and Janoff's Future Search principles (2010).

A district's transformation activities begin with one academic cluster and the central administration cluster. Both clusters organize and run Cluster Engagement Conferences, which are one- to three-day events. Each Cluster Redesign Team invites faculty and support unit staff within its cluster to participate in the conference. The purpose of the conference is to create a "fuzzy" idealized design (Ackoff, 2001; Banathy, 1991, 1992; Reigeluth, 1995) for each cluster. The idealized design must be aligned with the district's new strategic framework (mission, vision, and strategic goals) that was created during the earlier System Engagement Conference at the beginning of KWS Step 2. This idealized design must also frame in broad terms how the clusters will make simultaneous improvements along the three change-paths: Path 1—its relationships with external stakeholders, Path 2—its core and support work processes; and Path 3—its internal social infrastructure.

The Cluster Engagement Conferences are quickly followed by redesign workshops for both clusters. Each Cluster Redesign Team organizes these events for all of the schools and support work units within the clusters. Carefully selected faculty and staff from the schools and support work units participate in these workshops. The redesign workshops are organized using Emery's Participative Design Workshop principles (2006). The outcome of these events is a collection of recommendations for transforming each school or support work unit within the clusters.

The recommendations created in the redesign workshops are submitted to each Cluster Redesign Team who then organize the recommendations into a single proposal for transforming the environmental relationships, the core and support work processes, and the internal social infrastructure of each cluster and the schools and support units within the clusters. These proposals contain specific, actionable ideas for making simultaneous changes along the three change-paths identified earlier (i.e., each cluster's environmental relationships, work processes, and internal social infrastructure). Most importantly, the proposals must be unambiguously aligned with the system's grand vision and strategic direction.

After the first academic cluster and the central administration cluster have been engaged in their redesign activities and their effectiveness with the process has been evaluated, the remaining academic and nonacademic clusters join their system's transformation journey. The remaining clusters follow the same process as the first two clusters.

The number of change proposals created in KWS Step 2 will vary depending on the number of clusters within a district. It is appropriate and acceptable for each cluster to have different ideas for making improvements within their clusters. Allowing faculty and staff within each cluster to create innovative, but different, ideas for making improvements within their cluster is an example of applying the principle of equifinality (Cummings & Worley, 2001) to empower and enable the people who actually do the work of the district to make changes that make sense to them.

Although each cluster is encouraged to create innovative ideas for making simultaneous improvements along the three change-paths for their cluster, all of these improvements must be unequivocally aligned with the district's grand vision and strategic framework. To ensure this strategic alignment, the SLT reviews and approves all of the transformation proposals. Items marked for rejection or put on hold for a later implementation date must be negotiated with the CRTs that proposed them before those decisions are finalized. Items accepted for implementation are included in the final transformation proposal for each cluster.

In summary, the academic clusters invent ways to transform their environmental relationships, core and support work processes, and internal social infrastructure. The core work of the district is classroom teaching and learning. The core work process is embedded in the academic clusters. To be an effective district, all other work processes in the school system (the support work) must also be aligned with and supportive of the district's core work processes (i.e., classroom teaching and learning); therefore, the central office cluster is transforming at the same time as the first academic cluster to clearly and unequivocally support the changes that were proposed for the academic clusters.

The SLT now has redesign proposals from each of the academic clusters, the central office cluster, and the support work unit cluster. These proposals are consolidated into a master transformation proposal for the entire school system which is then submitted to the district's school board for review and approval.

Next, the SLT and Knowledge Work Supervisor have the challenging task of finding the money to implement the master transformation proposal. Earlier during the pre-launch preparation phase, the pre-launch team and the SLT scouted out funding opportunities by identifying some state and federal agencies or philanthropic organizations that could be sources of money to support their district's transformation journey. Now, they approach these agencies and organizations by submitting grant proposals requesting financial support. While waiting to secure outside money to support their transformation journey, they can kick-start the journey by reallocating money found within their district's current budget.

Money from outside agencies is often characterized as "extra" money because it is above and beyond the money in a district's normal operating budget. Even though extra money may be needed to sustain the first cycle of a transformation journey, money to kick-start a transformation journey can be found in the district's current operating budget using budget reallocation strategies. Further, future cycles of KWS should also be funded by permanent dollars in a district's budget. Additional information about how to pay for systemic change is found near the end of this chapter and in Duffy (2003).

Once the district has "seed" money to kick-start the transformation journey, the SLT distributes the financial, human, and technical resources to the CRTs so they can begin implementing their sections of the master redesign proposal. The CRTs delegate implementation responsibilities to the schools and support units within their domain. The implementation activities are managed on a daily basis by the schools and support work units and coordinated by the respective CRTs in collaboration with the Knowledge Work Supervisor. The SLT provides broad strategic oversight of the entire implementation phase.

Implementation of new ideas and practices will require the school system, all the clusters, all of the individual schools and work units, and all individual faculty and staff to move through a learning curve, which always starts with a downhill slide in individual and organizational performance followed by an upward climb toward excellence. This learning curve is characterized as a "first down, then up" principle (Kelly, 1999). Communities of Practice (COPs) can facilitate and support the "first down, then up" experience. COPs are informal groups of like-minded professionals who share common issues, problems, or opportunities related to the implementation of their district's master transformation proposal. They can be designed using DuFour and Eaker's principles for organizing learning communities (1998). The COPs are required to share their learning with everyone in the district to facilitate the development and dissemination of professional knowledge throughout the school system.

Most large-scale change efforts fail during the implementation period; especially if the change timeline is long and if the transformation activities and outcomes are not periodically evaluated (Sirkin, Keenan, & Jackson,

2005). Because of the possibility of failure, it is important for the various change-leadership teams to design and facilitate On-Track Seminars. On-Track Seminars are designed using Preskill and Torres's principles of evaluative inquiry (1998). The formative evaluation data from these seminars are used to keep the transformation journey on course toward the district's grand vision and strategic goals. These seminars also

- facilitate individual, team, and district-wide learning;
- educate and train faculty and staff to use inquiry skills;
- create opportunities to model collaboration, cooperation, and participation behaviors;
- establish linkages between learning and performance;
- facilitate the search for ways to create greater understanding of what affects the district's success and failure; and
- rely on diverse perspectives to develop understanding of the district's performance.

During the period of formative evaluation, it is important to assess the quality of discontent among people working in the school system and among key external stakeholders. The quality of discontent is a diagnostic clue about the relative success of a school system's transformation journey. If the transformation is not going well, people complain about little things—low-order grumbles. These gripes are manifestations of what Maslow called deficiency needs (cited in Farson, 1996, p. 93). If the transformation is succeeding, people have high-order gripes that focus on more altruistic concerns. In very successful transformation efforts, people engage in meta-gripes—complaints about their need for self-actualization. When change-leaders hear these meta-gripes, they will know that their system is likely succeeding with its transformation journey.

Step 3: Create Strategic Alignment

As a district's transformation journey unfolds, the KWS process transitions to Step 3: Create Strategic Alignment. During this phase the Knowledge Work Supervisor and Cluster Redesign Teams focus on aligning the work of individuals with the goals of their teams, the work of teams with the goals of their schools and work units, the work of schools and work units with the goals of their clusters, and the work of clusters with the goals of the district. Combined, these activities are referred to as strategic alignment.

Creating strategic alignment accomplishes three things (Duffy, 2004). First, it ensures that everyone is working toward the same broad strategic goals and vision for the district. Second, it weaves a web of accountabilities that makes everyone who touches the educational experience of a child accountable for his or her part in shaping that experience. And third, it has the potential to form a social infrastructure that is free of bureaucratic hassles, dysfunctional policies, and obstructionist procedures that limit individual and team effectiveness. It is these dysfunctional hassles, policies, and procedures that cause at least 80 percent of the performance problems that are usually blamed on individuals and teams (Deming, 1986).

Step 4: Evaluate Whole-System Performance

The performance of the entire transformed district is evaluated in Step 4 of the KWS methodology using principles of summative evaluation (see Stufflebeam, 2002, 2003). The purpose of this level of evaluation is to measure the success of everyone's efforts to transform the system's external relationships, core and support work processes, and internal social infrastructure in ways that will significantly improve the quality of education that every child—*every* child—receives. Evaluation data are also reported to stakeholders in the external environment to demonstrate the district's overall success with their transformation journey.

After change-leaders and their colleagues work through all four steps of KWS, they then focus on institutionalizing the successful changes by practicing continuous improvement at the district, cluster, school, team, and individual levels of performance. Then, after a predetermined period of stability and incremental improvements, they "step-up" again by moving to KWS Step 5. Achieving high performance is a lifelong journey for a school district.

IN ANTICIPATION OF "YES, BUT"S

Whenever KWS is presented to an audience predictably several key objections are voiced. These common objections and responses to them are presented below. It is very important for change-leaders and school public relations specialists to anticipate objections to whole-system change and then prepare well-crafted messages that preempt the objections. By anticipating and preempting the objections, initial resistance to change can be significantly reduced. Further, the best time to anticipate and preempt objections is during the pre-launch preparation phase of KWS.

**Objection #1: "Yes, This Is an Interesting Idea.
But Where Is It Being Used"?**

One of the greatest "innovation killers" in the history of mankind is captured in the question, "Where is this being used?" or its corollary, "Who else is doing this?" Can you imagine Senge (1990) being asked this question when he first proposed his Fifth Discipline ideas, or perhaps Cogan (1973) when he first described the principles of Clinical Supervision?

New ideas, by definition, are not being used anywhere, but they want to be used. However, being the first at doing anything, especially doing something that requires change with broad scope and deep scale demands a high degree of leadership courage, passion, and vision. Many change-leaders in education do indeed have the requisite courage, passion, and vision (Duffy, 2003) to be the first to try innovative ideas for creating and sustaining transformational change, but they don't know how to lead whole-system change. These heroic leaders need a change protocol especially designed to create and sustain whole-district change. KWS is that protocol.

New methodologies to create and sustain district-wide transformation are not perfect and they never will be. Educators should not even try to find a perfect methodology. Instead, they need to examine innovative methods for navigating whole-system transformation, study how they work, find glitches in the processes, and search for logical flaws in the reasoning behind the methods. Then, assuming that a method is based on sound principles for transforming whole systems, educators should then think about how they can modify the methodology to make it work for their districts.

Some educators, professors, consultants, and policymakers will read about whole-district transformation and say, "Impractical." Not only are the KWS core principles and change tools based on these principles practical, many of them are proven to work in school districts and other organizations throughout the United States (see Reigeluth, 2007) and the world (see Issan & Gomaa, 2010). So, if and when someone says that trying to transform an entire school system is impractical, they should be asked, "If other schools and school districts have used these principles effectively, why can't you?"

Some people will read this book and proclaim, "Wow, these ideas are really far out. They are way outside the box." It is my hope that readers will say this. If they do, this means I have succeeded in offering them some innovative ideas to think about and apply. And, if and when they see something that seems "way outside the box," they should ask, "If this idea is outside the box, what box are we in?" and, "Do we want to stay inside this box of ours?"

Objection #2: "Yes, This Is a Nice Idea. But, How Do We Pay for This?"

The second biggest innovation killer in the world is found in the question, "How do we pay for this?" Unlike traditional reform efforts, whole-system transformation cannot be sustained solely through small increases in operating budgets, nor can it be sustained with "extra" money from outside the district. Because systemic transformation touches all aspects of a school district's core operations, it imposes significant resource requirements on a district and demands a rethinking of the way current resources are allocated, as well as some creative thinking about how to use "extra" money (that is, money from external sources) that will be needed to jump-start systemic reform.

Because there seems to be a scarce amount of literature on financing whole-district change, innovative, ground-level tactics, methods, and sources are needed to help educators find the financial resources they need to transform their school systems into high-performing knowledge-creating systems. What follows are some insights about how to do this. These insights are explored more deeply in Duffy (2003).

Below, readers will find a brief presentation of some fundamental principles that are important for financing whole-district change. Many of these principles are advocated by school finance experts (Clune, 1994a, 1994b; Keltner, 1998; Odden, 1998). The fundamental principles are as follows:

- Think creatively about securing resources. Instead of saying "We can't do this, because ..." say, "We can do this. Let's be creative in figuring out how?"
- Embed the resources to support a whole-system transformation in the district's organization design.
- Develop a new mental model for financing school system improvement that creates innovative solutions to resource allocation challenges (Odden, 1998).
- Fund systemic transformation with real dollars that are a permanent part of the district's budget.
- Reallocate current operating money to support whole-district improvement (Keltner, 1998).
- Over time, reduce "extra" resources for whole-district transformation to near zero while increasing internal resources to support systemic transformation.
- As needed, combine federal funds in innovative ways to directly support district-wide transformation of teaching and learning.
- Focus on financing for adequacy rather than on financing for equity (see Clune, 1994a, 1994b).
- When seeking outside money, make sure that the requirements and goals of the funding agency do not conflict or constrain the vision and strategic direction of the district's transformation goals.
- Employ superior communication skills so all stakeholders recognize the true purpose of the budget reallocation strategy, how it will work, and what the benefits will be.

Objection #3: "Yes, Nice Idea, But We Can't Stop Doing What We're Doing."

Another important and significant obstacle to gaining support for whole-system change is that school districts have a core mission; that is, they must provide children with a required number of days of classroom teaching and learning as specified by each state's department of education. Given the complexity of whole-system change and given the time required to plan and implement system-wide change, some educators will object by saying, "Nice idea, but we can't stop doing what we're doing to participate in this kind of change process. We have to show up every day and teach kids."

Of course, this objection is based on the realities of life in school systems. That's why it is so difficult to respond to this objection. But there is a response and it is derived from the experiences of real people making real changes in complex organizations with core missions that cannot be ignored. The response to this objection is that the SLT and Knowledge Work Supervisor must create a parallel organization after the launch decision is made during the pre-launch preparation phase.

The concept of parallel organization is from the fields of organization theory and design and systemic change (Stein & Moss Kanter, 2002). A parallel organization which is sometimes called a "parallel learning structure" (Human Resource Development Council, date unknown) is a change management structure. The parallel organization is that collection of change navigation teams and change processes that are temporarily established to change an entire organization. It is created during the pre-launch preparation phase of KWS.

The parallel organization is created by temporarily "transferring" carefully selected and trained educators into the parallel organization, which is constructed using the various change-leadership teams and the KWS protocol. These people then design the new system by following the KWS protocol to create proposals to transform their system.

Educators not transferred into the parallel organization continue to operate under the current school system, thereby helping the district to achieve its core mission, that is, educating children. Even though they are performing within the boundaries of the current system, these educators are participating in communities of practice to help them learn the new knowledge and skills they will need to perform successfully in the transformed school system.

In Step 2 of the KWS protocol, a master redesign proposal is created. At some point during Step 2 that proposal is implemented. As it is implemented, the "old" system and the parallel organization merge to create a transformed system whereby the district continues to achieve its core mission, but it does so within the framework of a "new" system.

The transition from the current organization to the "new" organization is not easy. The transition period is a time of ambiguity, confusion, chaos, complexity, and great change. A school district's covert insurgents (the political group called adversaries characterized earlier) will work to undermine the transformation journey. External stakeholders will question the new vision and wonder about the knowledge and skills of the change-leaders. The "pedestrians" (the political group called fence-sitters) in the school system will sit on the sidelines and watch while offering no support. Given these challenges, change-leaders will need personal courage to stand their ground in the face of adversity. Their passion for the core mission of their district (educating their community's children) will give them the emotional energy they need to persist on the transformation journey. And their vision of an exciting, desirable future for the district will be the North Star guiding their district ever closer to that envisioned future.

Objection #4: "Yes, Nice Idea, But We Don't Need to Do This. We Are Already a Good School System."

Collins (2001) posited that "good is the enemy of great." The "we're already a good system" is a pernicious objection that prevents a school district from becoming even better than it is. In anticipation of this objection, change-leaders might consider telling the following story followed by an explanation of the "S-curve."

Near the end of World War II, propeller-driven airplane engines had reached the upper limit of their performance capacity. Design engineers could not figure out how to make the engines go faster or fly farther. No amount of tinkering with the engines (i.e., the old system) could increase the engines' capacity. So, what did the design engineers do? They started thinking outside the box and they created a brand-new engine design—the jet engine; that is, they created a brand new system that was substantially different from the old system.

The jet engine system has now reached the upper limit of its performance capacity. Design engineers are now creating a brand-new system for powering planes. It's the rocket plane. Design engineers envision planes taking off in one place, traveling through space, and then landing in another place. Passengers will embark on a horizontal takeoff aboard a special rocket plane, climb to 40,000 feet before rockets fire, accelerate to 3,500 miles per hour, coast for a few minutes of weightlessness 62 miles above the Earth, flip over, and then return to ground—a feat that no current jet engine can achieve.

Like the airplane engines described in the above story, all systems have life cycles and all systems eventually hit the upper limits of their performance capacites. Handy (1995) and Branson (1987) both discuss the nature of system life cycles. They graphically depict system performance as an S-curve. As a system's performance matures, it approaches and eventually bumps up against an upper performance limit (this upper limit is often characterized as a "performance ceiling") and then the system starts to decline. Systems, however, can skirt along their performance ceilings for years, and while doing that, they will be perceived as "good" systems. However, at some point they will start to decline and no amount of tinkering with the old "good" system can prevent this decline in performance.

There is a way, however, to break through the performance ceiling to prevent system decline. It's called transformation. To avoid the downward slope of the S-curve, a different kind of intervention is required. The different intervention is to transform—to create a brand-new system (like the design engineers did for airplane engines) that allows the system to break through its performance ceiling to achieve new levels of performance.

Our nation's school systems are functioning as "old" systems. No amount of tweaking, no amount of piecemeal change, no amount of restructuring of the old system, and no amount of "band-aid" quick fixes will significantly improve the performance of those systems because they are either bumping up against the limits of their performance ceilings or they are on the slippery downward slope of the S-curve toward extreme dysfunction.

So, even though a school system may be "already good," the system can become a "great" one by breaking through the performance ceiling that is constraining its performance capacity, which will eventually bend the system's performance curve toward the downward tail of the S-curve. Systems break through their performance ceilings by transforming.

Objection #5: "Yes, Nice Idea, But It Will Take Too Much Time."

Transformational change does take time. In fact, it probably takes more time than we can ever imagine, and this time requirement forces change-leaders to look for the quick fix. They want changes that can be made today, tomorrow, next week, and next month. When told that transformational change may take years, if people respond by saying that "it takes too long," that statement is a hidden "no, we don't want to do that."

Another problem associated with the desire for quick fixes is that they rarely permanently solve the problems to which they are applied. In fact, research on systems dynamics by Kim and Lannon (1997) tells us that while a quick fix might create the illusion of problem dissolution, the original problem almost always returns and becomes worse.

Although transformational change takes more time than piecemeal, school-based reforms, the process can and should be expedited. As Miles (2010, online) noted, "Transformation launches must be bold and rapid to succeed." Managing the process so that it proceeds at a reasonable rate of speed, while simultaneously taking the time to make the necessary transformational changes, requires change-leaders who are masters of the art and science of transformation.

Objection #6: "Nice Idea, But We Don't Have the Right People Working in the System to Do This."

This objection seems to be rooted in a lack of confidence in the vision for the future of a school system or the change-leaders' lack of confidence in their ability to lead transformational change. But, who are the right people? The "right" people are the educators currently working in school systems who know that the old Industrial Age paradigm is failing, who see the promise of a new paradigm of personalized education, and who have the courage to speak out and speak up about their vision for the future of their school systems. The right people are the ones who will

- spread the word about the promise of transformation;
- build political support for change;
- seek out resources for change;
- influence others to think about change; and
- take the initiative instead of waiting for others to do so.

CONCLUSION

Teachers are knowledge workers and school systems are knowledge-creating organizations. The effectiveness of teachers as knowledge workers is inextricably connected to their professional intellect; that is, their effectiveness is connected to what they know and how they communicate what they know to their students.

The KWS methodology is designed to shift the focus of instructional supervision off individual teachers and on to the performance of entire school systems. KWS is a change methodology that can be used to transform a school system to help it break through to higher levels of performance by making significant changes to the system's (1) relationship with its external environment, (2) core and support work processes, and (3) internal social infrastructure.

KWS is also designed around contemporary change theory and principles. Contemporary change theory is based on the concept of flux. It recognizes that change is nonlinear and requires school districts to function at the edge of chaos as educators seek controlled disequilibrium to create innovative opportunities for improvement. Contemporary change theory tells us that

- to improve the performance level of a school district, the system must first move downhill before it can move up to a higher level of performance;
- to be an effective school system, that system must create a networked social infrastructure where innovations are grown from within and used to create whole-district change;
- to be an effective school system, that system must be able to anticipate the future and respond quickly to unanticipated events;
- to create transformational change, educators must use a change protocol specifically designed for that purpose; and
- an effective change process requires change-leadership to be distributed throughout a school district.

KWS also requires change-leaders who are courageous, passionate, and visionary and who use their power and political skills in ethical ways. Leaders like this are priceless and absolutely necessary. Leaders of this class work their magic by helping others to see the invisible, to do the seemingly impossible, and to create new realities heretofore only imagined. Creating world-class school districts that produce stunning opportunities for improving student, faculty and staff, and whole-system learning can only be done under the stewardship of these kinds of transformational leaders.

Leading whole-system change is not for the timid, the uninspired, or the perceptually nearsighted. It requires personal courage, passion, and vision. It is my hope that readers will find in the pages of this chapter and the rest of the book the key that unlocks or reinforces their personal courage, passion, and vision to lead this kind of large-scale transformation journey in their school districts. If they do step forward to accept that mission, they step forward into a world that is not fully illuminated by research findings, into a world that is a minefield of sociopolitical warfare and turf battles, and into a world where they will often suffer emotional pain and feelings of betrayal by those they thought loyal. They may even lose their jobs. But, with courage, passion, and vision they can create a coalition of like-minded change-leaders within and outside their districts, and in collaboration with this coalition they can develop the capacity to endure the pain and betrayal, move forward toward their shared vision for their districts, and ultimately succeed in creating and sustaining previously unimagined opportunities for improving student, faculty and staff, and whole-system learning in their school systems.

REFERENCES

Ackoff, R. L. (2001). *A brief guide to interactive planning and idealized design*. Retrieved on March 19, 2006, from: http://www.sociate.com/texts/AckoffGuidetoIdealizedRedesign.pdf.

Banathy, B. H. (1991). *Systems design of education: A journey to create the future*. Englewood Cliffs, NJ: Educational Technology.

Banathy, B. H. (1992). The prime imperative: Building a design culture. *Educational Technology, 32*(6), 33–35.

Beer, M., Eisenstat, R. A., and Spector, B. (1990). Why change programs don't produce change. *Harvard Business Review, 68*(6), 158–166.

Being First. (2006). How to build a critical mass of support to accelerate your change. Retrieved on April 22, 2006, from: http://www.beingfirst.com/resultsfromchange/pastissues/200212.php#3.

Block, P. (1986). *The empowered manager: Positive political skills at work*. San Francisco: Jossey-Bass.

Branson, R. K. (1987). Why schools can't improve: The upper limit hypothesis. *Journal of Instructional Development, 10*(4), 15–26. DOI: 10.1007/BF02905307. Retrieved on April 10, 2016, from: https://www.researchgate.net/publication/226660067_Why_schools_can't_improve_The_upper_limit_hypothesis.

Clune, W. (1994a). The shift from equity to adequacy in school finance. *Educational Policy, 8*(4), 376–394.

Clune, W. (1994b). The cost and management of program adequacy: An emerging issue in education policy and finance. *Educational Policy, 8*(4), 365–375.

Cogan, M. L. (1973). *Clinical supervision*. Boston: Houghton Mifflin.

Collins, J. (2001). *Good to great*. New York: Harper Business.

Cummings, T. G. and Worley, C. G. (2001). *Organization development and change* (7th ed.). Cincinnati, OH: South-Western College.

Deming, W. E. (1986). *Out of the crisis*. Cambridge, MA: Massachusetts Institute of Technology, Center for Advanced Engineering Study.

Drucker, P. F. (1985). *Management: Tasks, responsibilities, practices*. New York: Harper & Row.

Drucker, P. F. (1993, November/December). Professionals' productivity. *Across the Board, 30*(9), 50.

Drucker, P. F. (1995). Managing in a time of great change. New York: Truman Talley Books/Dutton.

Duffy, F. M. (1995). Supervising knowledge-work. *NASSP Bulletin, 79*(573), 56–66.

Duffy, F. M. (1996). *Designing high performance schools: A practical guide to organizational reengineering*. Delray Beach, FL: St. Lucie Press.

Duffy, F. M. (2003). *Courage, passion and vision: A guide to leading systemic school improvement*. Lanham, MD: Scarecrow Education and the American Association of School Administrators.

Duffy, F. M. (2004). *Moving upward together: Creating strategic alignment to sustain systemic school improvement*. No. 1, Leading Systemic School Improvement Series. Lanham, MD: Scarecrow Education.

Duffy, F. M., Rogerson, L. G., and Blick, C. (2000). *Redesigning America's schools: A systems approach to improvement*. Norwood, MA: Christopher-Gordon.

DuFour, R. and Eaker, R. (1998). *Professional learning communities at work: Best practices for enhancing student achievement*. Bloomington, IN: National Education Service.

Emery, F. E. (1977). *Two basic organization designs in futures we are in*. Leiden, the Netherlands: Martius Nijhoff.

Emery, M. (2006). *The future of schools: How communities and staff can transform their school districts*. Leading Systemic School Improvement Series. Lanham, MD: Rowman & Littlefield.

Farson R. (1996). *Management of the absurd*. New York: Simon & Schuster.

Handy, C. M. (1995). *The empty raincoat: Making sense of the future*. London: Random House Business Books.

Human Resource Development Council (date unknown). *Parallel learning structures*. Retrieved on March 26, 2006, from: http://www.humtech.com/opm/grtl/ols/ols6.cfm.

Issan, S. and Gomaa, N. M. M. (2010). *Knowledge Work Supervision: Transforming Omani schools into learning organizations*. Retrieved on April 30, 2016 from: http://www.ncpeapublications.org/attachments/article/41/m34266.pdf.

Karr, J-B. A. (date unknown). *Jean-Baptiste Alphonse Karr*. Retrieved on March 17, 2006, from: http://www.reference.com/browse/wiki/Jean-Baptiste_Alphonse_Karr.

Kelly, K. (1999). *New rules for the new economy*. New York: Penguin Books.

Keltner, B. R. (1998). *Funding comprehensive school reform. Rand Corporation*. Retrieved on January 15, 2004, from: http://www.rand.org/publications/IP/IP175/.

Kim, D. H. and Lannon, C. P. (1997). *Applying systems archetypes*. Waltham, MA: Pegasus Communications.

Kotter, J. P. (1996). *Leading change*. Boston, MA: Harvard Business School Press.

Langer, E. J. (1997). *The power of mindful learning*. Reading, MA: Addison-Wesley.

Learning Point Associates. (date unknown). *Teacher quality*. Retrieved on April 9, 2006, from: http://www.ncrel.org/policy/feature/tq.htm.

Lewin, K. (1951). *Field theory in social science*. New York: Harper & Row.

Miles, R. H. (2010, January-February). Accelerating corporate transformations (Don't lose your nerve!). *Harvard Business Review*. Retrieved on April 10, 2016, from: https://hbr.org/product/accelerating-corporate-transformations-dont-lose-your-nerve/an/R1001C-PDF-ENG.

Odden, A. (1998, January). *How to rethink school budgets to support school transformation*. Getting better by design, 3. ERIC Number: ED450478. Available from: http://files.eric.ed.gov/fulltext/ED450478.pdf.

Owen, H. (1993). *Open Space Technology: A user's guide*. Potomac, MD: Abbott.

Owen, H. (1991). *Riding the tiger: Doing business in a transforming world*. Potomac, MD: Abbott.

Pasmore, W. A. (1988). *Designing effective organizations: The socio-technical systems perspective*. New York: Wiley & Sons.

Pava, C. H. P. (1983). *Managing new office technology: An organizational strategy*. New York: The New Press.

Preskill, H. and Torres, R. T. (1998). *Evaluative inquiry for learning in organizations*. Thousand Oaks, CA: Sage.

Purser, R. (1991). *Redesigning knowledge work. The FULCRUM Update: Newsletter of the Fulcrum Network for Human Systems Development*. Rohnert Park, CA: The Fulcrum Network, Department of Management, Sonoma State University.

Quinn, J. B., Anderson, P., and Finkelstein, S. (1996, March-April). Managing professional intellect: Making the most of the best. *Harvard Business Review, 74*(2), 71–80.

Reigeluth, C. M. (2007). *Journey toward excellence: A systemic change effort in the Metropolitan School District of Decatur Township, Indianapolis, Indiana*. Retrieved on December 29, 2015, from: http://www.indiana.edu/~syschang/decatur/the_change_effort.html.

Reigeluth, C. M. (1995). A conversation on guidelines for the process of facilitating systemic change in education. *Systems Practice, 8*(3), 315–328.

Rhodes, L. A. (1997, April). Connecting leadership and learning. Arlington, VA: American Association of School Administrators. Unpublished manuscript.

Senge, P. (1990). *The fifth discipline: The art & practice of the learning organization*. New York: Doubleday.

Sirkin, H. L., Keenan, P., and Jackson, A. (2005, October). The hard side of change management. *Harvard Business Review*, 1–10.

Stein, B. A. and Moss Kanter, R. (2002). *Building the parallel organization: Creating mechanisms for permanent quality of work life*. Retrieved on March 25, 2006, from: http://www.goodmeasure.com/site/parallel%20org/index.htm.

Stufflebeam, D. L. (2002). *CIPP evaluation model checklist: A tool for applying the fifth Installment of the CIPP Model to assess long-term enterprises*. Retrieved on March 30, 2006, from: http://www.wmich.edu/evalctr/checklists/cippchecklist.htm.

Stufflebeam, D. L. (2003). *The CIPP model for evaluation*. Retrieved on March 30, 2006, from: http://www.wmich.edu/evalctr/pubs/CIPP-ModelOregon10-03.pdf.

Trist, E. L., Higgin, G. W., Murray, H., and Pollack, A.B. (1963). *Organizational choice*. London: Tavistock.

Weisbord, M. R. (2004). *Productive workplaces: Organizing and managing for dignity, meaning, and community*. San Francisco: Jossey-Bass.

Weisbord, M. R. and Janoff, S. (1995). *Future Search: An action guide to finding common ground in organizations and communities*. San Francisco: Berrett-Koehler.

Weisbord, M. R. and Janoff, S. (2010). *Future Search: Getting the whole system in the room for vision, commitment, and action*. San Francisco: Berrett-Koehler.

Chapter Two

Core Concepts, Principles, and Tools Underpinning Knowledge Work Supervision

Kevin McClellan, Division Manager for CharterAir (in Salter, 1998), was quoted as saying, "We didn't invent the truck, the plane, the phone, the computer, or the satellite. But we did put them together" (p. 126). In much the same way, I didn't invent sociotechnical systems (STS) design, Open Space Technology (OST), Future Search Conferences, Participative Design Workshops, learning organizations, communities of practice, quality improvement methods, or organization development methods, but I did put them together to create Knowledge Work Supervision (KWS). KWS is unique and innovative because of this combination of ideas and methods and because it is specially designed to transform entire school systems. There is no other instructional supervision or system improvement process that combines as many effective and powerful organization improvement tools and processes for the purpose of transforming entire school systems as KWS does.

KWS was created in the 1990s (Duffy, 1995a, 1995b, 1996, 1997a, 1997b). It was created by combining under one conceptual umbrella innovative ideas and methods for transforming professional work (aka knowledge work) with effective organization transformation principles and tools borrowed from several interrelated areas. Rogerson and Blick (in Duffy, Rogerson, & Blick, 2000) added new insights and concepts to the basic KWS approach that increased its effectiveness and power. The core concepts, principles, and tools that comprise KWS are summarized in this chapter.

BASIC PROPOSITIONS UNDERPINNING KNOWLEDGE WORK SUPERVISION

Underlying Propositions

The following propositions underlie Knowledge Work Supervision:

Proposition 1: The basic unit of change within a school system is a cluster of interconnected schools and support work units (e.g., central administration departments) rather than individual schools or work units. KWS focuses on making changes within each cluster that are aligned with and supportive of the strategic direction of the entire school system. This principle is reinforced in the literature on systemic transformation (see Pasmore, 1988, 1992).

Proposition 2: Effective transformation requires the use of the principles of systemic change. Transformation efforts will more likely produce system-wide excellence when principles of large-scale systemic transformation are consistently applied.

Proposition 3: The ideal design of each cluster is not preordained by what has worked in other districts at other times. Instead, the ideal design is defined by three broad characteristics: (1) those conditions under which the clusters are able to meet the changing demands of the larger turbulent environment which includes the broader school system, the organization culture, technology, finances, and the neighborhood(s) served by the cluster (by making improvements to the system's environmental relationships); (2) what it will take for each cluster to deliver excellent services to the "customers" within its purview (by making improvements to their core and support work processes); and (3) by the conditions under which the learning needs of teachers, administrators, and other staff are to be met (by making improvements to the system's social infrastructure).

Proposition 4: The transformation of the social infrastructure of a school system from a bureaucratic design to a democratic design is critical to the success of knowledge-creating systems staffed with knowledge workers. This transformation requires the chartering and ongoing support of work teams. Further, these teams must be empowered with real authority and responsibility for redesigning their relationship with the broader environment, their core and support work processes, and their social infrastructure and trained to use their new authority (i.e., they must be empowered and enabled).

Proposition 5: KWS improvements must be clearly aligned with the school system's strategic direction and coordinated to ensure ongoing strategic alignment.

Proposition 6: The new organization design created through KWS should facilitate practitioners' timely access to high-quality information and knowledge, allow them to influence decisions, and give them the authority to take appropriate actions so they can learn together to create shared knowledge about teaching and learning.

Proposition 7: The various clusters within a school system, the individual schools and departments within each cluster, and the many communities of practice within and among clusters need to be clearly linked and coordinated to support the strategic direction of the school system. Otherwise, the system is a confederacy of loosely connected parts rather than an interdependent system working toward common goals.

Proposition 8: Systems and individuals have low tolerance for multiple, yearly, rapid-fire changes. KWS improvements should be stabilized and allowed to stay in place for a predetermined period of time, as long as they continue to produce desired outcomes.

Proposition 9: Even though systemic stability is reestablished after completing the KWS transformation journey, none of the improvements should be viewed as necessarily permanent. The school system must seize opportunities in and deal with threats from its environment. This necessity requires school systems to maintain their capacity for future change.

Proposition 10: Practitioners must have a clear understanding of how to align their individual behavior with the school system's strategic direction. During KWS Step 3, individuals, teams, schools, and communities of practice are held accountable for behavioral alignment and are rewarded accordingly.

Proposition 11: A "healthy" school system is one that benefits the people within it and has a positive future. The guiding purpose of KWS is to transform entire school systems in ways that increase the value of these systems for the people they serve as well as to increase the likelihood that the school systems will evolve and flourish in the twenty-first century as high-performing knowledge-creating systems.

THE KNOWLEDGE BASE FOR KWS

KWS is born of the literature and successful practices of several interrelated areas: STS design (Emery & Trist, 1972; Hanna, 1988; Lytle, 1991; Pasmore, 1988, 1992; Pasmore, Francis, Haldeman, & Shani, 1982; Trist, 1969; Trist, Higgin, Murray, & Pollack, 1963), quality improvement (Crosby, 1979; Deming, 1982; Ishikawa, 1985; Juran, 1989; Taguchi & Clausing, 1990), organization development (Argyris & Schön, 1978; Burke, 1982; French & Bell, 1978; Senge, 1990), and knowledge work (Drucker, 1993; Knights, Murray, & Willmott, 1993; Pava, 1983a, 1983b, 1986). Key concepts and methods from each of these areas are described below.

Below, I summarize major conceptual building blocks for KWS: STS design, team-based organization design, bureaucracy to democracy in school systems, organization development, learning organizations, and communities of practice. I also provide an overview of key tools that are used with KWS: Future Search Conferences, Participative Design Workshops, and OST.

Core Concepts and Theories

Knowledge Work

KWS assumes that school districts are knowledge-creating systems, that teachers and support staff are knowledge workers, and that the process of enhancing professional intellect must be managed. Knowledge work uses information to produce new knowledge, design products, or deliver services.

Knowledge work has five components: quality information, key people who participate in an exchange of this information, varied forums for exchanging this information, effective technological devices to support the work, and high-quality work procedures and organizational functions (adapted from Pava, 1983a). Knowledge-creating systems also have an intricate social infrastructure composed of organization design, organization culture, quality of work life, and communication processes, among others.

The organization's social infrastructure is inextricably connected to the organization's core and support work processes. Knowledge-creating systems also exist within a broader environment and the organizations' relationships with the external environment affect the quality and effectiveness of their core and support work processes and their internal social infrastructure. Simultaneous changes must be made in all three areas to transform their districts into high-performing knowledge-creating systems.

Knowledge work uses information to produce knowledge, design products, or deliver services. Knowledge work includes teaching. Drucker (1993) noted that in 1880, about nine out of ten workers made and moved things. Today that ratio is down to one out of five. The other four out of five workers, he said, are knowledge workers. These workers converse on the phone, write reports, solve problems, create innovative designs, educate others, and attend meetings. Drucker (1985) posited that the central social problem of our new, Knowledge-Age society is to make knowledge work productive and knowledge workers achieving. Because teachers' knowledge is the "tool" they use to do their jobs, they are knowledge workers.

A significant portion of knowledge work happens inside a professional's head. It is the thinking that occurs so professionals can do their jobs effectively and with a high degree of quality. Drucker (1995) alluded to nature of knowledge work when he said, "knowledge workers own the tools of production. ... Increasingly, the true investment in the knowledge society is not in machines and tools. It is in the knowledge of knowledge workers" (p. 246).

Knowledge work in school districts occurs in the heads of teachers and is manifested primarily as teaching behavior. Knowledge work is nonlinear in nature. Nonlinear work consists of activities that can be done in parallel, separated from each other, or in a variety of sequences. In nonlinear work processes, future work cannot be decided until some results of the current work activities are completed. Consequently, we often experience nonlinear work as chaotic. There is no research evidence suggesting that this kind of knowledge work can be improved throughout an entire school system using traditional supervisory models (e.g., clinical supervision or supervision as performance evaluation).

Work processes that are linear and sequential support knowledge work. A linear work process is a sequence of steps that must be followed so that step one is completed before beginning step two, and so on. This process is "..the total collection of processes, procedures, instructions, techniques, tools, equipment, machines, and physical space used to transform the organization's inputs into the desired outputs (products or services). 'X' is transformed into 'Y' by doing 'Z'" (Lytle, 1991). In a school district, the supportive linear work process is the instructional program, often organized as prekindergarten through twelfth grade, within which students must complete first grade before moving into second grade, and so on. Resources (inputs) are poured into the instructional program with the intention of providing students with a high-quality education (desired outputs).

Practitioners improve the linear instructional program by auditing that work process to identify where mistakes are made, or where potential for mistakes exists; for example, by using a curriculum mapping tool. Then, they take actions to correct the mistakes or to eliminate the possibility of making them. However, in my opinion, the Industrial Age design of the traditional instructional program must be transformed—not reformed or reengineered—to provide children with a personalized learning experience.

Improving nonlinear knowledge work in schools, on the other hand, requires different actions. Remember that knowledge work in school districts occurs primarily inside the heads of teachers and it is manifested in their classroom teaching. Remember, too, Drucker's characterization of knowledge work: "knowledge workers own the tools of production. ... Increasingly, the true investment in the knowledge society is not in machines and tools. It is in the knowledge of knowledge workers" (1995, p. 246). The broad actions needed to enhance the professional intellect of knowledge workers are as follows(adapted from Pava, 1983):

- Improve the quality and timeliness of key information teachers need to teach effectively.
- Ensure that teachers interact with the key people with whom they should be exchanging critical information.

- Provide teachers and key people with a variety of structured, semistructured, and informal forums for exchanging information (e.g., in structured communities of practice, workshops, informal "brown bag" lunches, or national conferences).
- Examine and improve any devices (e.g., computers), work procedures (e.g., lesson planning), and organizational functions (e.g., traditional administration and supervision) that support teaching.

Quinn, et al. (1996) offered additional steps that can be taken to enhance professional intellect:

- Recruit the best (select the best applicants to fill positions), where best means those with highly desirable knowledge, skills, and dispositions.
- Force intensive early development (require people to engage in intensive early professional development activities).
- Constantly increase professional challenges (use job enrichment strategies to increase people's challenges).
- Evaluate and weed (evaluate performance and remove low performers).
- Boost professionals' problem-solving abilities by capturing knowledge in systems and software (create an organization-wide knowledge management system).
- Overcome professionals' reluctance to share information (e.g., create communities of practice and require participants to share their learning).
- Organize around intellect (empower people to create customized solutions to problems they experience at work).
- Invert the system's organization design (i.e., turn the hierarchical pyramid upside down and put teachers at the top and senior administrators and other support personnel at the bottom).
- Create intellectual webs (encourage and support the formation of self-organizing communities of practice staffed by like-minded people who share a common interest or work task).

KWS provides a systemic and systematic model for enhancing and managing professional intellect in school systems.

Professional Intellect

The primary tool of knowledge workers is their professional intellect, a concept expanded upon by Quinn, Anderson, and Finkelstein (1996). Quinn et al. said, "The capacity to manage human intellect—and to convert it into useful products and services—is fast becoming the critical executive skill of the age" (p. 71). Further, these authors said that professional intellect operates at four levels: *cognitive knowledge* (knowing what to do), *advanced skills* (knowing how to do it), *systems understanding* (knowing why it must be done), and *self-motivated creativity* (caring about why it should be done) (p. 72). I believe that professional intellect must be managed in school systems to provide teachers with the knowledge and skills they need to design effective learning environments for students.

Sociotechnical Systems Design

The field contributing the most to the foundation of KWS is STS design. The key concept borrowed from STS design is that organizations are complete systems with components that interact with each other and which exist within a broader environment. The system functions by converting "inputs" into "outputs." Inputs are human, financial, and technical resources used to do work (using a conversion process) inside the organization that results in products or services (outputs) being delivered to a customer. "Feedback" (i.e., the results of an evaluation of the quality and timely delivery of a product or service) is provided to managers and employees working in the organization so they can improve what they are doing.

STS theory originated at the Tavistock Institute of Human Relations. Its use has spread quickly to most industrialized nations (Cummings & Worley, 2014). STS theory suggests that whenever people are organized to perform tasks (such as in a school system), a joint system is created composed of two separate but related subsystems: a technical subsystem composed of the tools, techniques, and methods people use to get the job done (which I refer to as core and support work processes) and a social subsystem that includes organization design, organization culture, the reward system, and the relationships between and among people doing their work (which I describe as the internal social infrastructure).

The Technical Subsystem

This subsystem consists of the tools, techniques, and methods people use to convert resources into a product or service that is delivered to a customer or client in the external environment. The technical system is not just the equipment that is used—it also includes the work processes, procedures, or tasks. It is the core and support work processes of an organization. In school systems, the technical subsystem is the teaching-learning process in classrooms conjoined with the linear instructional program that is often organized as a pre-K—12th grade process. The technical subsystem in school districts also contains support work processes such as the central administration, building and grounds maintenance, pupil personnel services, and transportation services.

A key concept used to understand and improve the technical subsystem is variance. Variances are errors in the work process. The most important errors are called key variances. Major events in an organization's environment can cause or increase the strength of these variances.

One commonly observed phenomenon in work processes is that upstream variances (errors) flow downstream and cause problems later on in the work process (Pasmore, 1988). A good example of this phenomenon in school systems was given to me by a high school principal who invited me to his school to make a presentation about supervising knowledge work. When I mentioned "upstream errors causing downstream problems," the principal interjected by saying "I know exactly what you mean. That's happening right here in our district. Our middle school curriculum is being 'dumbed down.' Those kids are coming to us unprepared for our more rigorous high school curriculum. That 'upstream error' is flowing downstream right to us and causing a whole bunch of problems for us."

The Social Subsystem

Hellriegel, Slocum, and Woodman (1998, p. 599) paraphrased Pasmore (1988) who characterized the STS approach as focusing simultaneously on "changing both the technical and social aspects of the organization" as a means to "optimize their relationship and thus increase organizational effectiveness." Hellriegel et al. continued by saying:

> The STS approach regards the organization as more than just a technical system for making products and providing services. Ultimately, the organization is a collection of human beings—a social system. Changes made by the technical system affect the social fabric of the organization (Hellriegel, et al. 1998, p. 599).

The social subsystem also involves the division of labor and methods of coordinating work (Lawrence & Lorsch, 1967). Division of labor defines how tasks are assigned or how organization roles are staffed. Once work is divided up it has to be coordinated. Organizations use a variety of coordination methods. The most common coordinating mechanism is hierarchy. Another method for coordinating work is the use of rules and regulations. A major element of coordination is the informal, unwritten code of conduct (behavioral norms) that spells out how people are supposed to interact.

The social subsystem must also engage people. Without a strong commitment to high-performance, carelessness, inattention, and alienation will undermine even the most sophisticated work process (Walton, 1980). Therefore, those who transform school systems must build in features that evoke and sustain commitment and involvement. Examples of these features were identified by Emery and Thorsrud (1976). They called these features "psychological job criteria." These criteria are

- autonomy and discretion;
- opportunity to learn and continue learning on the job;
- optimal variety;
- opportunity to exchange help and respect;
- sense of meaningful contribution; and
- prospect of a meaningful future.

As noted earlier, my name for the social subsystem is social infrastructure. In addition to the elements described above, the social infrastructure of a school system also includes critical skills associated with a particular job, organization culture, communication structures and processes, the reward system, and organization design (e.g., a mechanistic design vs. an organic design).

In traditional manufacturing organizations, the two subsystems—social and technical—are independent of each other in the sense that they operate according to two discrete sets of behavioral principles (Cummings & Worley, 2014). The social subsystem is influenced by biological and psychosocial principles. The technical system (which contains the core and support work processes of an organization) functions according to mechanical and physical principles.

In knowledge-creating systems the mechanical and physical variables associated with traditional manufacturing systems are mitigated by biological, psychological, and social variables. This is why traditional system redesign interventions (like restructuring) that require a detailed analysis of variances (errors or the potential for errors) in a sequential manufacturing work process don't work effectively for improving knowledge work. Although knowledge workers often use tools, methods, and techniques that come under the influence of mechanical and physical principles, their main tools and work processes are their personal knowledge, interpersonal and team communication, and the thinking process they use to get the job done. Knowledge work is primarily subject to behavioral and psychosocial principles—not mechanical and physical principles.

New ways of defining and improving the technical system are required in knowledge organizations where the core and support work processes are guided by principles of knowledge work. Pava (1983a, pp. 92–110) proposed four actions for improving knowledge work:

- Improve the quality and timeliness of information and knowledge that the knowledge worker needs to do his or her job effectively.
- Provide knowledge workers with access to others who have the information and knowledge they need.

- Provide many opportunities for exchanging information and knowledge with key others.
- Improve the quality and effectiveness of devices (equipment used to support knowledge work) and organization functions designed to support knowledge work (like administration).

The social subsystem and the technical subsystem have separate outcomes. The technical subsystem yields products and services. The social subsystem results in social and psychological outcomes such as job satisfaction, motivation, morale, and level of commitment to the organization's goals (Beer, 1980). An important challenge for transforming school systems is to redesign the relationship between these two subsystems so they work well together and so that each produces positive outcomes. This concern for improving both subsystems is called "joint optimization" (Cummings & Worley, 2014). The quality of products and services increases and the level of human satisfaction increases as both subsystems work well together and produce positive outcomes.

The System's External Environment

The second major premise of the STS design approach is that organizations as systems are open to their environments (Cherns, 1987; Cummings & Srivasta, 1977; Trist, Higgin, Murray, & Pollack, 1963). The environment provides organizations with the resources needed to perform. The organization provides the environment with products and services. Those who want to redesign their school systems for high performance need to figure out how to improve the interface between the organization and its environment so that the organization maintains sufficient freedom to do what it needs to do while interacting effectively with its environment. The process for structuring and improving an organization's relationship with its environment is called boundary management. Principles of boundary management are built into the KWS approach.

The external environment of a school system has a significant and unique impact on that system. More than any other organization, school systems are the subject of never-ending demands from external stakeholders. Sometimes these demands are unrealistic, yet nevertheless powerful. The local business community, teachers' unions, state legislative actions, teacher preparation programs, professional associations, and the federal government, as well as parents and students themselves, all provide specific inputs and expect certain (often contradictory) outcomes from school systems. This tension requires school systems that are adaptable to the expectations of their environment yet firm in their resolve to accomplish their ultimate mission: providing youngsters with an excellent and equitable education that teaches them the attitudes, concepts, and skills needed to function effectively in our twenty-first-century democratic society.

Some Final Words on STS Design

STS interventions are used in a variety of settings, including manufacturing firms, hospitals, schools, and government agencies (Cummings & Worley, 2014). The implementation of STS interventions requires high worker participation in the work design and implementation process. Participative work design (Emery, 1977; Emery & Purser, 1995) allows workers to use their professional intellect to create innovative ideas for redesigning their organizations. This high level of participation creates a sense of ownership of the redesign ideas and implementation plans. When workers feel they own (ownership is related to the psychological principle of efficacy) the redesign process, they tend to be highly committed to implementing the work designs (Weisbord, 1984). KWS is a high-involvement approach for redesigning entire school systems.

Team-Based Organization Design

Setting priorities and providing resources are not enough to transform entire school districts into high-performing knowledge-creating systems. Senior- and school-level managers must actively support and encourage the transformation of their school systems from a traditional hierarchical organization design into a democratic, self-managing team design. Substantial research also exists on the effectiveness of self-managed teams (Goodman, Devadas, & Hughson, 1988). The team-based design also creates high-involvement opportunities for faculty and staff to help shape and lead their district's transformation. High involvement is a significant factor affecting the overall success of a transformation effort.

One of the core principles of KWS is that work teams take responsibility for getting the job done, for figuring out what improvements are needed, for determining how the improvements should be made, and for evaluating how performance can be further improved. Further, a team is a special type of group organized, regulated, and defined through its communication processes. These communication processes are framed and shaped by the team members' commitment to a shared vision. A self-managed team is designed to address the needs of a complex task by creating its own work processes, rules for accountability, and definitions of specific outcomes.

KWS has five key players: a pre-launch team, a Strategic Leadership Team (SLT), Cluster Redesign Teams, and Communities of Practice (COPs);

the fifth key player is the linchpin that orchestrates all these teams, the Knowledge Work Supervisor (each of these roles are described in more detail in chapter 3). As networked teams, these key players not only work within their team boundaries, they also communicate across team boundaries.

KWS teams are self-managing, yet coordinated to produce systemic transformation. None of the teams act in isolation. The coordinating mechanisms (e.g., the Knowledge Work Supervisor role, horizontal and vertical communication structures, and computer-based knowledge management systems) built into KWS harness the power of teams to produce systemic transformation.

In KWS, various change-leadership teams are responsible for coordinating and improving the core and support work processes within their purview. These teams must strive to create unity of effort to achieve system-wide goals for providing children with an excellent and equitable education. The Knowledge Work Supervisor, as the linchpin, orchestrates this unity of effort.

Bureaucracy to Democracy in School Systems

Because KWS requires a high level of participation, the traditional bureaucratic organization design of school systems should be replaced with a participative organization design. It is impossible to have a high degree of participation and ownership within bureaucratic operating principles.

High participation is one of the critical factors for successful transformation. MacMullen (1996) reviewed and analyzed factors affecting improvements made in schools that were part of the Coalition of Essential Schools. MacMullen concluded that a significant requirement for successful reform is the inclusion of the whole faculty in developing the strategic direction of the school system. Similarly, Peterson, McCarthey, and Elmore (1996) learned through their research that successful school restructuring was related to teachers working together as a whole staff or in teams. Fullan (1991) recommended the "redesign [of] the workplace so that innovation and improvement are built into the daily activities of teachers" (p. 353)—a recommendation that implied the need for a high level of teacher participation in the school improvement process.

High participation also contributes to a sense of self-efficacy; that is, the sense that one has some degree of influence or control over something. Rosenholtz (1989) found that teachers with a strong sense of efficacy were more likely to adopt new classroom behaviors and were more likely to stay in the profession. McLaughlin and Talbert (1993) confirmed Rosenholtz' findings. They suggested that giving teachers opportunities for learning together results in a body of teaching wisdom that could be widely shared. Darling-Hammond (1996) commented on how this level of teacher collaboration and participation is rare, yet the need for it, she said, is greater now than at any time in the past.

There is a growing emphasis on increasing participation even in the business world where bureaucratic organization designs have stifled employee participation. The work of Senge (1990), Block (1993), Galagan (1994), and Whyte (1994), among others, emphasized the importance of collectively engaging all staff in vision building, identifying problems, learning, and finding creative solutions to challenging problems. Increasing the participation of faculty and staff in a school system's internal social infrastructure is one of the key outcomes of KWS and it begins during KWS Step 1. This outcome has to be fully understood before beginning KWS because the success of systemic transformation depends on it—low participation or no participation means no transformation.

The transformation from a bureaucratic to democratic organization design is keyed to two design principles conceived by Emery (1977) and Emery and Purser (1995). They described in detail how these two basic principles capture the essential characteristics of organization design. Emery and Purser argued that these two basic design principles largely determine the outcomes of all organization redesign efforts. The first, called Design Principle 1 (DP1), is based upon "top-down" bureaucratic assumptions about how human systems should be organized and managed. The second, Design Principle 2 (DP2), is based upon "worker-centered" participation as the foundation for designing and managing organizations. These two opposing design principles, and their inherent assumptions about "optimizing" human systems, lead practitioners down very different paths for system transformation. KWS requires DP2.

Design Principle 1

If an organization's environment remains relatively constant and if the organization doesn't have to adapt to its environment then a bureaucratic design is appropriate (Burns & Stalker, 1961). However, when the environment is unstable and when adaptation to the environment is required bureaucratic organizations are literally unable to adapt effectively to the demands of their environment.

The primary technology that links knowledge workers together is communication. Any organization structure that inhibits, impedes, or distorts communication will effectively prevent knowledge workers from accomplishing their tasks. Bureaucratic hierarchy (DP1), with the main purpose of controlling communications and relationships, actually constrains the creativity and flexibility needed to adapt to the changing needs of stakeholders and the environment.

Bureaucratic organization design also has inherent dysfunction built into it. Bureaucratic designs do not reward honesty, teamwork, or flexibility among organization members. Other dysfunctional effects of the bureaucratic design (DP1) are summarized below (from Emery & Purser, 1996, pp 128–129):

- Communication across functions is rare because workers only focus on their areas.
- Workers mostly provide information that makes them look good.
- It's in no one's interest to provide accurate or timely feedback.
- Competitive structures emerge—person against person, group against group.
- Workers feel divested from the outcomes of their work, are only aware of and rewarded for a small piece of the product, and, therefore, have little commitment to product quality.
- Informal "shadow" groups or cliques form to meet worker needs for control, belonging, and self-worth.

Design Principle 2

School system transformation influenced by the bureaucratic DP1 is flawed because those making the changes institute more of the same bureaucracy. Instead, what is needed is a new organization design based on DP2 (democratic, self-managing principles). Common and fundamental flaws of past school improvement efforts (e.g., top-down problem-solving, using outside consultants to analyze the system and prescribe improvements, and narrow redesigns that are site-based rather than system-based) are direct consequences of applying the bureaucratic design principle (DP1). DP1 is ill-adapted and ill-advised in systems such as school districts that may require rapid responses to environmental changes, flexibility in implementing changes, a high degree of ownership for results, and methods that can be replicated internally without overly relying on costly external experts.

The democratic, self-managing organization design (DP2) promotes organization strengths needed by today's school systems and effectively uses the skills of knowledge workers who make schooling successful. The effects of DP2 are summarized below (from Emery & Purser, 1996, pp. 130–132):

- There is mutual support and respect among team members.
- Communication and feedback among team members is direct and timely.
- Workers learn and develop across functions; variety is increased as workers share functions.
- Workers set their own goals in the context of system requirements.
- Each worker takes responsibility for the whole product.
- Workers are invested in the outcome of the product; they have a sense of working together to produce the whole and are therefore committed to production quality.

Carmichael (1982) wrote about building principals being perceived as all-wise and all-competent because of their perceived power and authority (a perspective anchored to the bureaucratic organization design—DP1). Kleine-Kracht (1993) offered a different view of principals. She recommended that administrators and teachers must be learners that engage in collaborative "questioning, investigating, and seeking solutions" (p. 393) for school improvement (a perspective anchored to the democratic organization design—DP2). Kleine-Kracht also observed the traditional perspective that "teachers teach, students learn, and administrators manage is completely altered ... [There is] no longer a hierarchy of who knows more than someone else, but rather the need for everyone to contribute" (p. 393) (this is an example of the DP2 principle). A democratic organization design (DP2) provides a context for administrators and teachers to learn and grow collaboratively and to view themselves as "all playing on the same team and working toward the same goal."

Organization Development

Another field that contributed to the development of KWS is organization development. There are many concepts from this field that contributed to the design of KWS. Change theory, large-scale change, fast-cycle change, conflict management, managing resistance to change, decision-making, problem-solving methods, and so forth, all contributed to the design of KWS. Two key concepts from this field summarized below are "learning organizations" and "communities of practice."

Learning Organizations

One significant contribution from the field of organization development is the notion of the "learning organization." Argyris and Schön (1978) wrote much about this concept. However, it was Senge (1990) who popularized the phrase "learning organization" in his book *The Fifth Discipline*.

Senge described learning organizations as places "where people continually expand their capacity to create the results they truly desire, where new and expansive patterns of thinking are nurtured, where collective aspiration is set free, and where people are continually learning how to learn together" (Senge, 1990, p.1). Garvin (1993) described a learning organization as "an organization skilled at creating, acquiring, and transferring knowledge, and at modifying its behavior to reflect new knowledge and insights" (p. 80).

The hallmarks of a learning organization, according to Senge, are skills for

- systematic problem solving;
- experimenting with new approaches;
- learning from their own experience;

- learning from the experiences of others; and
- transferring knowledge quickly and efficiently throughout the organization.

KWS offers a way to transform entire school systems into learning organizations. It is comprehensive, systematic, systemic, and strategic; it aims to create and use new approaches to schooling; it creates processes for a school district to learn from this experience; it provides opportunities for key players to exchange critical information with others; and it is designed to transfer knowledge quickly throughout a school district.

Communities of Practice

An idea that spun out of the learning organization literature is the concept of communities of practice. A COP is a network of practitioners collaborating to learn how to do their jobs better, to solve common problems, or to create innovative ideas.

A COP is established when practitioners from different levels and with different responsibilities work together collaboratively and continually to improve the quality of their work and the quality of work life. This kind of collaboration is grounded in what Newmann (cited in Brandt, 1995) and Louis and Kruse (1995) called reflective dialogue. Educators who are part of a professional COP engage in reflective dialogue about students, teaching, learning, and other aspects of their responsibilities; for example, Sergiovanni (1996) said, "If our aim is to help students become lifelong learners by cultivating a spirit of inquiry and the capacity for inquiry, then we must provide the same conditions for teachers" (p. 52). Creating and supporting COPs provides teachers with the capacity for and spirit of collaborative inquiry and learning.

COPs require supportive conditions that determine when, where, and how educators and support staff can collaborate as a network to learn, make decisions, solve problems, and redesign their work. There are two types of conditions needed to support COPs: physical conditions and human capacities (Boyd, 1992; Louis & Kruse, 1995).

The physical conditions. Louis and Kruse (1995) discussed the physical conditions needed to support COPs. These are as follows: (1) time to meet and talk, (2) small size of a school and physical proximity of staff to one another, (3) teaching roles that are interdependent, (4) communication structures, (5) school autonomy, and (6) teacher empowerment. Donahoe (1993) argued that rearranging the use of time in schools so staff can collaborate is a prime issue to be resolved when restructuring schools. Raywid (1993) also addressed the need for providing meaningful time for collaboration and learning.

The human capacities. Louis and Kruse also discussed the human capacities needed to support COPs. A basic human capacity needed for creating effective

COPs is a willingness to accept feedback and make improvements. Additional human capacities include respect and trust among colleagues, possession of professional knowledge and skills for effective teaching and learning, supportive leadership, and an intensive socialization process within the system.

Lee, Smith, and Croninger (1995) reported the results of an extensive study of school restructuring that was conducted by the Center on Organization and Restructuring of Schools. Their study included 11,000 students enrolled in 820 secondary schools across the United States. In the schools where the COP concept was employed, the staff collaborated to change their teaching. These changes engaged students in higher-level intellectual learning tasks. Students achieved greater academic gains in math, science, history, and reading than did their counterparts in traditionally organized schools. Additionally, the achievement gaps between students from different backgrounds were smaller in the "learning community" schools.

The Center on Organization and Restructuring of Schools (Newmann & Wehlage, 1995) conducted four research studies of restructuring schools where the learning community concept was in place. These studies used rigorous three- and four-year longitudinal research methods combined with survey data and the analysis of student achievement data. The studies collected data on 1,500 elementary, middle, and high schools throughout the United States. Additionally, field research was conducted in forty-four schools in sixteen states. The results of this research suggested that the comprehensive redesign of schools, including decentralization, shared decision making, schools within schools, teacher teaming, and/or professional communities of staff can improve student learning (Hord & Boyd, 1997).

Although the research suggests that COPs are powerful structures for improving teaching and learning, it must be remembered that simply chartering these networks doesn't guarantee positive outcomes. McLaughlin (1993) made this point when she cautioned that professional communities, by themselves, are not necessarily good things. That which makes the difference between an effective COP and an ineffective one is the focus of the group. If a COP has misplaced values and beliefs that do not support the overall transformation of the school system then chances are the COP will be ineffective.

CORE KWS TOOLS

Future Search Conferences

Future Search (Weisbord & Janoff, 2010) is a powerful large-group planning method used by communities, business, government, education, health care, nonprofit, and faith-based institutions. This tool is used at the beginning of KWS Step 2. The Future Search methodology is used to organize and run a System Engagement Conference. The System Engagement Conference enables participants to

1. collectively create a picture of a desired future for their school system;
2. bring faculty and staff together to discover the values, purposes, and projects they hold in common;
3. improve communication, learning, and collaboration;
4. improve strategic thinking;
5. improve relationships throughout the school system; and
6. lower resistance to change and increase levels of commitment to support system transformation.

Future Search Principles

A Future Search usually involves sixty to seventy people—large enough to include many perspectives and small enough that the participants can engage in dialogue. Participants do not need training or expertise to participate effectively in the conference. The optimal length for the conference is three days.

The conference is designed to enable participants to work together and explore strategic issues without defending a particular agenda. A key outcome of the conference is the creation of common ground in support of school system transformation.

The core Future Search principles are as follows:

- Get the "whole system" in the room—a cross section of people representing all parts of the school system who have the information, authority, resources, ability to act, and a stake in the success of the system.
- Global perspective and local action—ensure that all participants see and understand the transformation vision before deciding upon action.
- Focus on common ground and future action (not problems and conflicts)—treat conflicts and problems as information while creating common ground in support of the transformation.
- Self-managed small group dialogue and learning—consultants manage large group facilitation while participants apply principles of self-management within small-group conversations.

Participative Design Workshops

The participative design workshop (PDW) tool was also developed by Merrelyn and Fred Emery and described at length in *Participative Design for Participative Democracy* (Emery, 1993). The PDW is a process that engages people in designing and implementing a highly effective, self-managing work system. This approach recognizes that imposed change fails. To avoid failed transformation efforts, the PDW method involves teachers and support staff in creating innovative ideas for transforming their school district. The PDWs are used during KWS Step 2 and they are called redesign workshops.

Each academic and support work unit cluster organizes and runs redesign workshops for the faculty and staff in each cluster. The redesign workshops teach participants how to analyze (1) their current relationship with the external environment, (2) their core and support work processes, and (3) their internal social infrastructure. The outcome of the redesign workshops are innovative ideas for transforming the cluster's environmental relationships, core and support work processes, and internal social infrastructure. Then, each Cluster Redesign Team develops a detailed plan for implementing desired changes and for evaluating results within their cluster. These plans are then submitted to the SLT for review and approval.

Open Space Technology

OST (Owen, 1991, 1993) is a powerful method for engaging stakeholders from the external environment in a meaningful and productive dialogue about their relationship with a school system. OST is a large-group process that brings together a wide range of key stakeholders from a school system's environment to interact with members of the school district and explore critical issues in the relationship between the district and its environment. OST principles are used during KWS Step1 to design and run a Community Engagement Conference.

Most school districts find that a two- or three-day Community Engagement Conference will likely generate powerful and long-lasting positive effects. Previously unnoticed talent and energy for innovation emerges from the various stakeholders during the second and third days. The longer sessions also give sufficient time for issues to emerge which may not be initially obvious and allow conversations to generate creative ideas for the future.

Community Engagement Conferences are designed to generate maximum productive conversations and responsible future actions with minimal top-down direction. In keeping with this goal of maximum self-direction, the "Law of Two Feet" applies (Owen, 1991). This "law" states that if people are participating in a discussion that is not generating personal passion or interest, then those participants should use their two feet and move on to a discussion that catches their interest. Further, if the topics that people are concerned about are not being addressed it is their responsibility to bring them up. As Owen says "There is a time to talk and a time to walk. Sophistication is defined as knowing when" (p. 165).

A Community Engagement Conference is managed using the following principles (adapted from Owen, 1991, p. 164):

- "Whoever shows up are the right people." This reminds participants that having a 100 percent participation rate is not needed to make a difference. It is important, however, that the "right" people attend conference—people from the community with the knowledge, energy, passion, and commitment required to support the school system's transformation journey.
- "Whatever happens is the only thing that could have happened." This reminds participants that the outcomes of the Community Engagement Conference cannot be predicted.
- "Whenever it starts, this is the right time." This reminds participants that creativity and innovation are not easily kept to a schedule. Innovations emerge from conversations among the right mix of people, ideas, methods, and enthusiasm.
- "When it's over, it's over ... and when it isn't over it isn't over." This reminds participants that on one hand people have a limited amount of energy to participate in discussions. At the same time, some discussions will become energized and quite productive and these should not be shut down because of time limits.

Participants who volunteer to lead discussions around a particular topic of interest take responsibility for creating a record of the key discussion points. These notes can be submitted to a central location where specially trained staff enter the information into a computer database. Additionally, computer records can keep track of who is willing to take an active role in making innovation happen following the event. During multiday Community Engagement Conferences all of the computer-generated "reports" can be printed out and distributed to all participants.

The desired outcome of a Community Engagement Conference during KWS Step 1 is to generate ideas, passion, and commitment to help the school system create a better future for the students it teaches, the faculty and staff who work in the system, and for the community it serves. This conference helps define broad educational issues that are important for a wide cross-section of people from the community; that is, stakeholders from the external environment. These issues provide invaluable "front-end" information for the System Engagement Conference that is organized later for school system faculty and staff at the beginning of KWS Step 2.

CONCLUSION

I believe that KWS is a powerful method for transforming entire school systems with a focus on supervising knowledge work processes. KWS is powerful because it

- combines for the first time effective concepts and methods from several different but interrelated fields;
- transforms the social infrastructure of a school system from a bureaucratic design to a democratic one;
- uses innovative methods for analyzing and improving three sets of key school system variables: its relationship with its broader environment, its core and support work processes, and its internal social infrastructure;
- uses a high-involvement strategy to engage educators in a collaborative effort to improve the quality of education in their systems;
- charters and supports COPs;
- shifts the focus of instructional supervision off individual teachers onto the school system's environmental relationships, core and support work processes, and internal social infrastructure;
- coordinates transformational change activities until the entire school system is transformed into a high-performing knowledge-creating system; and
- is used for the life of a school district—KWS is a never-ending upward spiral that moves an entire school system toward higher and higher levels of performance.

This chapter concludes Section 1. In this section, I provided a glimpse of a vision for an innovative supervisory process called KWS that is designed to transform entire school systems. I also summarized key concepts, principles, and tools that are part of KWS.

Section 1 also provided a theoretical foundation for KWS—it was the "what" and the "why" section. It was a cognitive map of the terrain that change-leaders need to traverse. In Section 2, I provide a "compass" (practical advice about when, where, and how to use KWS) and I serve as an expert guide through this challenging territory called systemic transformation.

REFERENCES

Argyris, C. and Schön, D. (1978). *Organizational learning.* Reading, MA: Addison-Wesley.

Beer, M. (1980). *Organization change and development: A systems view.* Santa Monica, CA: Goodyear.

Block, P. (1993). *Stewardship: Choosing service over self-interest.* San Francisco: Berrett-Koehler.

Boyd, V. (1992). *School context: Bridge or barrier to change?* Austin, TX: Southwest Educational Development Laboratory.

Brandt, R. (1995, November). On restructuring schools: A conversation with Fred Newmann. *Educational Leadership, 53*(3), 70–73.

Burke, W. W. (1982). *Organization development: Principles and practices.* Boston: Little, Brown.

Burns, T. and Stalker, G. M. (1961). *The management of innovation.* London: Tavistock.

Carmichael, L. (1982, October). Leaders as learners: A possible dream. *Educational Leadership, 40*(1), 58–59.

Cherns, A. (1987). Principles of sociotechnical design revisited. *Human Relations, 40,* 153–162.

Crosby, P. B. (1979). *Quality is free: The art of making quality certain.* New York: New American Library.

Cummings, T. G. and Srivasta, B. (1977). *Management of work: A sociotechnical systems approach.* San Diego: University Associates.

Cummings, T. G. and Worley, C. G. (2014). *Organization development & change* (10th ed.). Cincinnati: South-Western College.

Darling-Hammond, L. (1996, March). The quiet revolution: Rethinking teacher development. *Educational Leadership, 53* (6), 4–10.

Deming, W. E. (1982). *Out of crisis.* Cambridge, MA: MIT.

Donahoe, T. (1993, December). Finding the way: Structure, time, and culture in school improvement. *Phi Delta Kappan, 77*(1), 19–21.

Drucker, P. F. (1985). *Management tasks, responsibilities, practices.* New York: Harper & Row.

Drucker, P. F. (1993, November- December). Professionals' productivity. *Across the Board, 30* (9), 50.

Drucker, P. F. (1995). *Managing in time of great change.* New York: Truman Tally Books/Dutton.

Duffy, F. M. (1995a). Designing high-performance schools through instructional supervision. ERIC Clearinghouse. EA026350.

Duffy, F. M. (1995b). Supervising knowledge work. *NASSP Bulletin, 79*(573), 56–66.

Duffy, F. M. (1996). *Designing high-performance schools: A practical guide to organizational reengineering.* Del Ray Beach, FL: St. Lucie.

Duffy, F. M. (1997a, January). Knowledge Work Supervision: Transforming school systems into high-performing learning organizations. *International Journal of Educational Management, 11*(1), 26–31.

Duffy, F. M. (1997b, May). Supervising schooling, not teachers. *Educational Leadership, 54*(8), 78–83.

Duffy, F. M., Rogerson, L. G., and Blick, C. (2000). *Redesigning America's schools: A systems approach to improvement.* Norwood, MA: Christopher-Gordon.

Emery, F. E. (1977). *Two basic organization designs in futures we are in.* Leiden: Martius Nijhoff.

Emery, F. E. and Thorsrud, E. (1976). *Democracy at work: The report of the Norwegian industrial democracy program.* Leiden: Martius Nijhoff.

Emery, F. E. and Trist, E. L. (1972). *Toward a social ecology: Contextual appreciation of the future in the present.* London: Plenum.

Emery, M. (Ed.). (1993). *Participative design for participative democracy.* Canberra, Australia: Australian National University.

Emery, M. and Purser, R. E. (1995). *The search conference: A comprehensive guide to theory and practice.* San Francisco: Jossey-Bass.

Emery, M. and Purser, R. E. (1996). *The search conference: A powerful method for planning organizational change and community action.* San Francisco: Jossey-Bass.

French, W. L. and Bell, C. H., Jr. (1978). *Organization development: Behavioral science interventions for organization improvement.* Englewood Cliffs, NJ: Prentice Hall.

Fullan, M. with Stiegelbauer, S. (1991). *The new meaning of educational change.* New York: Teachers College Press.

Galagan, P. (1994, December). Reinventing the profession. *Training and Development,* 48(12), 20–27.

Garvin, D.A. (1993, July-August). Building a learning organization. *Harvard Business Review,* 71(4), 78–91.

Goodman, P., Devadas, R., and Hughson, T. (1988). Groups and productivity: Analyzing the effectiveness of self-managing teams. In J. Campbell and R. Campbell (Eds.). *Productivity in organizations.* San Francisco: Jossey-Bass (pp. 295–325).

Hanna, D. P. (1988). *Designing organizations for high performance.* Reading, MA: Addison-Wesley.

Hellriegel, D., Slocum, J. W., Jr., and Woodman, R. W. (1998). *Organization behavior (8th ed.).* Cincinnati, OH: South-Western College.

Hord, S. M. and Boyd, V. (1995, Winter). Staff development fuels a culture of continuous improvement. *Journal of Staff Development,* 16(1), 10–15.

Ishikawa, K. (1985). *What is total quality control? "The Japanese way."* Englewood Cliffs, NJ: Prentice-Hall.

Juran, J. M. (1989). *Juran on leadership for quality.* New York: The Free.

Kleine-Kracht, P. A. (1993, July). The principal in a community of learning. *Journal of School Leadership,* 3(4), 391–399.

Knights, D., Murray, F. and Willmott, H. (1993). Networking as knowledge work: A study of strategic interorganizational development in the financial services industry. *Journal of Management Studies,* 30(6), 975–995.

Lawrence, P. R. and Lorsch, J. W. (1967). *Organization and environment.* Cambridge, MA: Harvard University Press.

Lee, V. E., Smith, J. B., and Croninger, R. G. (1995). Another look at high school restructuring. In *Issues in restructuring schools.* Madison, WI: Center on Organization and Restructuring of Schools, School of Education, University of Wisconsin-Madison.

Louis, K. S. and Kruse, S. D. (1995). *Professionalism and community: Perspectives on reforming urban schools.* Thousand Oaks, CA: Corwin Press.

Lytle, W. O. (1991). *Sociotechnical systems analysis and design guide for linear work.* Plainfield, NJ: Block-Petrella-Weisbord.

MacMullen, M. M. (1996). *Taking stock of a school reform effort: A research collection and analysis.* Occasional Paper Series #2. Providence, RI: Annenberg Institute for School Reform, Brown University.

McLaughlin, M. (1993). What matters most in teachers' workplace context. In J. W. Little and M. McLaughlin (Eds.). *Teachers' work: Individuals, colleagues, and contexts.* New York: Teachers College Press.

McLaughlin, M. W. and Talbert, J. E. (1993). *Contexts that matter for teaching and learning.* Stanford: Center for Research on the Context of Secondary School Teaching, Stanford University.

Newmann, F. M. and Wehlage, G. G. (1995). *Successful school restructuring.* Madison, WI: Center on Organization and Restructuring of Schools, School of Education, University of Wisconsin-Madison.

Owen, H. (1991). *Riding the tiger: Doing business in a transforming world.* Potomac, MD: Abbott.

Owen, H. (1993). *Open space technology: A user's guide.* Potomac, MD: Abbott.

Pasmore, W. A. (1988). *Designing effective organizations: The sociotechnical systems perspective.* New York: Wiley & Sons.

Pasmore, W. A. (1992). *Sociotechnical systems design for total quality.* San Francisco, CA: Organizational Consultants.

Pasmore, W. A., Francis, C., Haldeman J., and Shani, A. (1982). Socio-technical systems: A North American reflection on empirical studies of the seventies. *Human Relations, 32,* 1179–1204.

Pava, C.H.P. (1983a, Spring). Designing managerial and professional work for high performance: A sociotechnical approach. *National Productivity Review,* 126-135.

Pava, C.H.P. (1983b). *Managing new office technology: An organizational strategy.* New York: The New Press.

Pava, C.H.P. (1986). Redesigning sociotechnical systems design: Concepts and methods for the 1990s. *The Journal of Applied Behavioral Science, 22*(3), 201–221.

Peterson, P. L., McCarthey, S. J., and Elmore, R. F. (1996, Spring). Learning from school restructuring. *American Educational Research Journal, 3*(4), 356–379.

Quinn, J. B., Anderson, P. and Finkelstein, S. (1996, March-April). Managing professional intellect: Making the most of the best. *Harvard Business Review 74*(2), 71–80.

Raywid, M. A. (1993, September). Finding time for collaboration. *Educational Leadership, 51*(1), 30–34.

Rosenholtz, S. (1989). *Teacher's workplace: The social organization of schools.* New York: Longman.

Salter, C. (1998, September). Roberts rules the road. *Fast Company, 17,* 114–128

Senge, P.M. (1990). *The fifth discipline: The art and practice of the learning organization.* New York: Doubleday.

Sergiovanni, T. J. (1996). *Leadership for the schoolhouse.* San Francisco: Jossey-Bass.

Taguchi, G. and Clausing, D. (1990). Robust quality. *Harvard Business Review, 68*(1), 65–72.

Trist, E. L. (1969). On socio-technical systems. In W. Bennis, K. Benne, and R. Chinn (Eds.) *The planning of change* (2nd ed.). New York: Holt, Rinehart, & Winston.

Trist, E. L., Higgin, G. W., Murray, H., and Pollack, A.B. (1963). *Organizational choice.* London: Tavistock.

Walton, R. E. (1980). Establishing and maintaining high commitment work systems. In J. R. Kimberly & R. H. Miles (Eds.). *The organizational life cycle.* San Francisco: Jossey-Bass.

Weisbord, M. (1984). Participative work design: A personal odyssey. *Organizational Dynamics,* 5–20.

Weisbord, M. and Janoff, S. (2010). *Future Search: Getting the whole system in the room for vision, commitment, and action* (3rd ed.). San Francisco: Berrett-Koehler.

Whyte, D. (1994). *The heart aroused: Poetry and the preservation of the soul in corporate America.* New York: Doubleday.

Section 2

KNOWLEDGE WORK SUPERVISION PROTOCOL

In this section, I provide a detailed description of how to use the Knowledge Work Supervision (KWS) protocol. In chapter 3, readers learn more about the KWS key players and their roles. Chapter 4 dives into KWS Step 1: Pre-Launch Preparation—which is a very important phase of the KWS protocol. Chapter 5 focuses on KWS Step 2: Redesign the Entire System with a description of the process, tasks, tools, and goals. Chapter 6 discusses KWS Step 3: Create Strategic Alignment, a critical goal for sustaining and institutionalizing change. Chapter 7 focuses on KWS Step 4: Evaluate Whole-System Performance. Finally, in chapter 8, I discuss KWS Step 5: Recycle to Pre-Launch Preparation.

Chapter Three

The Key Players and Their Roles
Creating and Using the Power of Teams

In this chapter, I identify sets of broad competencies for each of the five key players in the Knowledge Work Supervision (KWS) methodology. I also describe a set of competencies for a transformed central administration office (which becomes a central service center). I do not define the specific attitudes, concepts, and skills that comprise each competency area because these will vary from district to district.

THE POWER OF TEAMS

One of the main obstacles to transforming school systems is hierarchy—the "gift" of the Industrial Age to our organizations, including school systems. To engage effectively in transformation activities, school systems need to use a team structure. One of the key features of KWS is the use of clusters of schools and support work units led by change-leadership teams to produce whole-system transformation. There are significant advantages to using teams to create transformational change:

- First, it has long been known that the people closest to the work know best how to improve it.
- Second, using teams and clusters increases participation and collaboration which, in turn, creates powerful conditions for motivation, job satisfaction, and commitment to the district and its goals.
- Third, teams break down hierarchical fire walls and create opportunities for cross-boundary communication and collaboration.
- Fourth, teams create the conditions needed to create and diffuse district-wide knowledge.

BROAD COMPETENCIES FOR EFFECTIVE KNOWLEDGE WORK SUPERVISION

I believe that the broad competencies described in this chapter do not exist in isolation. Instead, they interact dynamically to create effective transformational change. There is a significant body of research about "dynamic competencies" (Fiol, 1991; Reed & DeFillipi, 1990). Lei, Hitt, and Bettis (1996) suggested that simply acquiring knowledge is insufficient for developing core competencies. Mitchell (1988) said, "Competence emerges when a person's talents, skills, and resources find useful application in meeting a commensurate challenge, problem, or difficulty" (p. 48). This interaction between knowledge acquisition and application is what Lei et al. (1996) referred to as "dynamic competencies."

Core competencies for a particular job are not held by a single individual. Rather these competencies are distributed across various roles within an organization. In other words, no single job performer possesses or demonstrates all of the competencies required to transform a school system. This observation suggests that individuals don't possess critical competencies for organizational success—teams do. Within the context of KWS, it also implies that developing competencies is an ongoing endeavor as teams continuously strive to develop and expand the specific attitudes, concepts, and skills associated with each set of dynamic competencies.

THE KEY PLAYERS

There are five key players for effective KWS:

1. The pre-launch team.
2. The Strategic Leadership Team (SLT).
3. The Knowledge Work Supervisor.
4. Cluster Design Teams.
5. Communities of Practice (COPs).

A brief description of each player is provided below.

CORE COMPETENCIES FOR THE KWS KEY PLAYERS

Competencies Need Context

Whitaker (1996) stated that "context" is a state-of-the-art issue for systems theory. Context is the specific situation within which action occurs. The context for organized teaching and learning is a school system, the individual schools and classrooms within that system, and the external environment that contains that system. Effective performance requires a supportive context. Having a set of competencies but no context within which to use them incapacitates the competencies. For example, imagine having the ability to paint beautiful landscapes, but not having access to canvas, paints, brushes, and so on. What good would it do to have those painting skills but not have a context for using them? The KWS competencies, like painting skills, also require a context. The context for the KWS competencies is a school system within a supportive external environment that is "ready" to engage in systemic transformation.

Core Competencies

Duffy and Reigeluth (2008) identified ten change leadership competencies for the "FutureMinds: Transforming American School Systems" initiative that they codirect. They believe that leaders who want to facilitate systemic transformational change must

1. have strong interpersonal and group facilitation skills;
2. have a positive mindset about empowering and enabling others to participate effectively in a transformation journey;
3. have experience in pre-K–12 education;
4. have an understanding of the dynamics of complex systemic change and about how to create and sustain this kind of change;
5. have a personal presence and track record that commands respect;
6. have a likeable personality;
7. be organized;
8. be flexible and open-minded about how change occurs with ability to tolerate the messiness of the change process;
9. have a positive, can-do attitude; and
10. 1be creative thinkers.

Duffy and Reigeluth assumed that very few current leaders in America's school systems have all the requisite technical knowledge and skills they need to guide a school district's transformation journey (characteristic #4 above). But they do believe that there are many current education leaders who have all of the other characteristics listed above. However, while knowledge and skills can be taught, the other dispositions probably cannot be taught because they are functions of a person's personality, personal style, and who they are as people (i.e., personal presence, ability to command respect, likable personality, and a positive mind-set). However, I believe that these nontrainable dispositions can be enhanced and refined through professional development opportunities.

The Pre-Launch Team

Purpose

The purpose of this team is to explore the feasibility of launching a transformation journey for their school system. They do a quick scan of the external environment to identify trends, issues, threats, and opportunities in the external environment that may affect the school system. They also do a quick informal assessment of external and internal political support for transformation among external and internal stakeholders. Given this information, they build a case for launching a transformation journey.

Membership

Each school system must decide how to staff this team. The only nonnegotiable permanent member of the team is the school superintendent. The staffing pattern shown below is only an example:

1. Superintendent.
2. Assistant Superintendent.
3. An influential teacher.
4. The teacher union president.
5. Others as determined by the superintendent.

Functions

This team completes an early assessment of their system's readiness to change, assesses the level of political support that is currently available, forms an SLT, and organizes a Community Engagement Conference.

The Strategic Leadership Team

Purpose

The SLT provides broad leadership for the transformation of their school system into a high-performing knowledge-creating system. The SLT does not replace the superintendent as the CEO of the school district. Instead, the SLT assists him or her in managing school system transformation.

Membership

The SLT is composed of the superintendent of schools, a selection of his or her trusted assistants, influential teachers and building administrators from each level of schooling (elementary, middle, and secondary), and a

Knowledge Work Supervisor. Some school systems may include parents, students, or even a school board member.

A key criterion for membership on the SLT is that each member must support the goal of systemic transformation. This should be nonnegotiable. A second criterion for membership is that influential teachers and building-level administrators from within the clusters are selected by their colleagues, not by the superintendent. This also should be nonnegotiable. The reason for this criterion is that the SLT must be representative of system-wide interests, rather than administrative preferences. A second reason is that by asking cluster-level faculty and staff to appoint members to the SLT, change-leaders begin practicing principles of participation and collaboration that are key outcomes of the KWS methodology. However, these nominees must be supporters of transformation and possess the intellectual skills to participate effectively on the SLT.

The SLT is a permanent organization structure. The positions (not the people) on the team are permanent. Although the team structure is permanent, a rotation schedule for staffing the various positions should be created. The only positions with nonrotating membership are the positions of the superintendent and the Knowledge Work Supervisor (of course, if a district has a high turnover rate in the superintendent's office there will be de facto rotation). The nonrotating individuals must remain in their positions to provide district-level stability for the KWS process and it outcomes. All other positions could be staffed on a rotating basis with new members.

Although the superintendent has a permanent position on the SLT, the fact is that a school system might have a high turnover in the superintendent's office. The average job tenure for school superintendents in the United States is five to six years (American Association of School Administrators, 2006). This means that a district may see many new superintendents over the life of the district. If a district has high turnover in the superintendent's chair, then the district's school board might want to develop policies to protect the system's transformation journey from the vagaries of transient chief administrators. This approach to protecting hard-earned transformational change is a key tactic for sustaining and institutionalizing change.

Functions

The SLT is primarily responsible for providing broad oversight of their system's transformation journey starting in the later phases of KWS Step 1.

The SLT receives education (concept- and attitude-focused) and training (skill-focused) shortly after the team is formed in KWS Step 1. The superintendent's training and education in these areas starts earlier in Step 1 when the pre-launch team is formed. As new members rotate onto the SLT, "older" members need to educate the new members in each of the six competency areas. The education and reeducation of the SLT is important and must not be neglected. Training and education is ongoing.

Knowledge Work Supervisor

Purpose

The Knowledge Work Supervisor provides tactical leadership to ensure that the district's transformation journey stays on track and that all the changes are strategically aligned with the district's mission and vision. Some school districts may decide to appoint and train a cadre of Knowledge Work Supervisors. The Knowledge Work Supervisor is an "integrator" responsible for establishing and maintaining vertical and horizontal communication linkages between and among the various clusters within the district.

Why This Role Is Important

School system transformation must have a whole-system perspective. If, for example, a student's total educational experience is fourteen grades long (e.g., pre-K–12), it is both logically reasonable and functionally necessary to examine and improve the entire "stream" of grades as a "whole" experience. It is neither reasonable nor practical to make improvements in a middle school program separate from the elementary program that feeds into it and the high school program that comes after it. Likewise, it makes even less sense to improve what's happening inside individual schools as if they were not part of a pre-K–12 teaching/learning process. School district transformation must be systemic rather than piecemeal and all improvements must be connected to the district's mission, vision, and strategic direction.

If school district transformation must have a whole-system perspective, then it also seems logical to argue that coordinating this kind of comprehensive school district transformation process requires a special role. Someone needs to provide vertical and horizontal coordination of school district transformation. This "someone" is a Knowledge Work Supervisor.

Some school systems may choose to follow a different transformation goal—one that creates a paradigm shift in how they educate children. The paradigm shift that is often advocated is one that displaces the Industrial-Age pre-K–12th grade "assembly line" with an education paradigm built on principles of personalized learning (see Reigeluth & Karnopp, 2013). If this becomes the transformation goal then the role of the Knowledge Work Supervisor becomes even more important because paradigm shifting requires significant coordination and effort.

Cluster Redesign Teams

Purpose

An entire school system is the system targeted for transformation. The transformation process engages clusters of schools and support work units in the transformation journey. Cluster Redesign Teams (CRTs) provide leadership for redesigning their clusters.

Membership

Members of CRTs are influential and competent faculty and staff within the cluster. The people nominated to serve on these teams must be supporters of the transformation journey and they must have the intellectual capacity to perform effectively. Membership is set up on a rotating basis so that many members of the cluster can serve on this team.

Functions

A CRT is chartered and trained for each academic and support work cluster. This team's primary responsibility is to provide leadership for redesigning its cluster's environmental relationships, core and support work processes, and its internal social infrastructure. The CRTs also encourage and support the formation of COPs within their boundaries and across boundaries. Members of the teams are also responsible for preparing a comprehensive proposal to redesign their clusters. They review this proposal to ensure that it supports the mission, vision, and strategic direction of their cluster and the school district.

Communities of Practice

Purpose

COPs create and disseminate professional knowledge throughout a school system. They do this by forming, disbanding, and re-forming around professional issues, needs, or interests. The school system then requires these groups to share what they learn with others in the system.

Membership

There are three kinds of COPs. The first are intact work teams (e.g., a team of sixth grade teachers, bus drivers, cafeteria workers, or secretaries). The second are temporary "circles of learning" (e.g., a group of K–12 language arts teachers forming a study group that lasts for two semesters). Membership in the first kind is on the basis of team membership. Membership in the second kind is voluntary. Both kinds of "communities" may decide upon their own criteria for membership and participation. A third kind of COP is composed of a single teacher and his or her students as they collaborate to cocreate knowledge.

Functions

COPs are intended to give participants timely and frequent access to professional knowledge and opportunities to interact with people who have the knowledge they need, which are two of the criteria for improving knowledge work (Pava, 1983). These "circles of learning" can form around common needs, issues, or interests. The informal COPs last as long as they need to last. They can disband and re-form, or they can disband and never be heard from again. One important obligation for COPs is that whatever they learn together must be shared with others who have a need for that information. In this way, COPs are important building blocks for a school district's knowledge-creating process.

CONCLUSION

Within the context of KWS, teams—not individuals—possess critical core competencies important to the overall success of their schools, clusters, and school system. Developing these team-based competencies is also a lifelong journey. Team members will come and go. Current knowledge will become obsolete. Current skills will become outdated. Continuous learning is required to replace these competencies and to develop new ones. Finally, a transforming school system must design ways to manage the knowledge creation process to create and disseminate system-wide knowledge and skills.

REFERENCES

American Association of School Administrators (2006). Superintendent and District Data. Retrieved on January 15, 2016, from: http://www.aasa.org/content.aspx?id=740.

Duffy, F. M., and Reigeluth, C. M. (2008). The school system transformation (SST) protocol. Educational Technology, *48*(4), 41-49.

Fiol, C. M. (1991). Managing culture as a competitive resource: An identity-based view of sustainable competitive advantage. *Journal of Management, 17*, 191–211. DOI: 10.1177/014920639101700112.

Lei, D. Hitt, M. and Bettis, R. (1996). Dynamic core competencies through meta-learning and strategic context. *Journal of Management, 22*(4), 549–571. DOI:10.1016/S0149-2063(96)90024-0.

Mitchell, R. G. (1988). Sociological implications of the flow experience. In M. and I. S. Csikszentmihalyi (Eds.). *Optimal Experience*. Cambridge: Cambridge University Press.

Pava, C. H. P. (1983). *Managing new office technology: An organizational strategy*. New York: The New Press.

Reed, R. and DeFillippi. R. J. (1990). Causal ambiguity, barriers to imitation, and sustainable competitive advantage. *Academy of Management Review, 15*, 88–102.

Reigeluth, C. M. and Karnopp, J. R. (2013). *Reinventing schools: It's time to break the mold*. Lanham, MD: Rowman & Littlefield Education.

Whitaker, R. (1996). Managing context in enterprise knowledge processes. *European Management Journal, 14*(4), 399–406. DOI: 10.1016/0263-2373(96)00027-8.

Chapter Four

Step 1: Pre-Launch Preparation

Knowledge Work Supervision (KWS) Step 1: Pre-Launch Preparation is a critically important phase in the KWS methodology. It is important because it lays the foundation for a successful transformation journey. The phase should not be hurried thereby leading to insufficient preparation nor should it be so agonizingly slow that it quenches enthusiasm to transform a school system.

Early in Step 1, a small group of district leaders led by the superintendent make a commitment to explore their district's readiness to change. I call this group the "pre-launch team." Early indicators of a system's level of readiness to change are found in a set of four preconditions that need to exist within a school system prior to launching the pre-launch preparation phase. I cannot overstate the importance of these conditions. In the absence of these conditions a transformation journey will likely fail. The conditions are

- leaders who act on the basis of personal courage, passion, and vision, not on the basis of fear or self-survival;
- leaders who conceive of their school systems as whole systems, not as a collection of individual programs and activities;
- leaders and followers who have a clear view of the opportunities that transformation offers them, not a view of "we can't do this because ..."; and
- leaders and followers who have basic knowledge of the art and science of school system transformation, not people without an inkling about the requirements of navigating transformational change.

One of the key reasons for failed change is lack of well-conceived, comprehensive, and successfully completed pre-launch activities. Preparing a school system for large-scale transformation is the most critical phase of the entire KWS methodology. Just as a building must be constructed on a solid foundation, whole-system change must also be built on a solid foundation. This foundation prepares a school system to engage successfully in the transformation process. Change-leaders should avoid the temptation to seek the "quick fix" by rushing through Step 1. Change-leaders should also avoid the temptation of making the process so agonizingly slow that it feels like slogging through knee-deep mud.

Step 1 is a collection of activities that help change-leaders get ready to engage in whole-system change. The activities are outlined and then described below in more detail. It is tempting to imagine that these activities should be done in a sequential, step-by-step process. Although they can be implemented sequentially, it is likely that many of them could be implemented at the same time; for example, building internal and external support for the transformation could happen simultaneously. The key activities are as follows:

- Define the system to be transformed.
- Recognize needs and opportunities.
- Build external support for the transformation.
  - Identify key external stakeholders.
  - Confer with your state department of education.
  - Identify sources of external human, financial, and technical resources.
- Build internal support for the transformation.
  - Identify allies, opponents, bedfellows, adversaries, and fence-sitters.
  - Quantify the level of support and resistance.
- Identify possible sources of financial resources.
- Assess the system's readiness to change.
- Organize and conduct a Community Engagement Conference.
- Make a launch/don't launch decision.
- If the decision is to launch the transformation, then continue the pre-launch activities by organizing a change structure to support the transformation.
  - Form and train a Strategic Leadership Team (SLT).
  - Appoint and train one or more Knowledge Work Supervisors.
- At the end of the pre-launch preparation phase, educators will be ready to move to KWS Step 2.

DEFINE THE SYSTEM TO BE TRANSFORMED

In the language of systemic change the system to be transformed is called the "target system." Some people have a difficult time conceptualizing what a system is, which causes them to look at their school district as a collection of semi-independent, unconnected, or loosely connected parts. Others have a penchant for defining the target system so broadly that it makes the thought of engaging in a transformation journey so complex and cumbersome that educators give up before they even start to transform their school system (e.g., a school system plus its community plus colleges and universities plus state departments of education plus the profession of education represents the target system in some people's minds).

A simple, practical, and realistic method for identifying the target system is to write the words "Our School District" on a large piece of flip chart paper and then draw a circle around it. Everything inside the circle is the target system. Everything outside the circle is the system's external environment.

The external environment has an impact on the school system, so change-leaders need to identify major stakeholders in the environment. They do this using the same piece of flip chart paper referred to above. Outside the circle representing their system they identify their system's major suppliers (e.g., local colleges and universities with teacher preparation programs, suppliers of equipment and materials) and their major customers (i.e., school-age children and their parents). They also list the names of other stakeholders who influence, care about, or rely upon the outcomes of schooling in their district; for example, the state department of education. The map will be used later in the pre-launch phase to conduct a stakeholder analysis.

RECOGNIZE NEEDS AND OPPORTUNITIES

Most practitioners are skilled at identifying needs and then using those data to plan for change. Focusing only on identifying needs, however, is an incomplete planning philosophy. Change-leaders must also identify opportunities that can be seized if action is taken. This dual focus on needs and opportunities creates a push-pull psychological dynamic; that is, focusing on needs pushes people to change while focusing on opportunities pulls people toward change. To create and complete successful transformation efforts change-leaders need to create this push-pull dynamic.

Needs and opportunities are identified using a process called environmental scanning. An environmental scan is a process for identifying needs and opportunities in the external environment that could affect a school system's transformation journey. The pre-launch team scans the environment by paying attention to what's happening in the education profession, economic conditions, federal and state legislation, local tax changes, forces for and against change, and so on. The results of the scan are used to conduct a Strengths, Weaknesses, Opportunities, and Threats (SWOT) analysis.

The SWOT analysis is a technique to analyze environmental scan data to identify threats to the school system and opportunities that might benefit the system. To conduct a SWOT analysis the pre-launch team creates a SWOT

Table 4.1 SWOT Matrix

	Opportunities	Threats
Strengths	What strengths does our system have that can help us seize these opportunities?	What strengths do we have that can help us minimize or avoid these threats?
Weaknesses	What weaknesses does our system have that might prevent or hinder us from seizing these opportunities?	What weaknesses do we have that make us more vulnerable to these threats?

matrix like the one shown in table 4.1. Then, as a team they reach consensus on the probability of each threat and opportunity having an effect on their system. Next, they reach consensus on their system's ability to eliminate or ameliorate the threats and seize the opportunities by identifying the system's strengths and weaknesses.

BUILDING EXTERNAL AND INTERNAL SUPPORT FOR TRANSFORMATION

The pre-launch team now returns to the system map they constructed earlier—the large piece of flip chart paper with the words "Our School District" inside a large circle and a list of major stakeholders outside the circle. Using the map, they now begin an assessment of their key external stakeholders' expectations, issues, and suggestions, as well as their predicted level of influence on the system.

Stakeholder expectations, issues, and suggestions can be collected using an interview process. Members of the pre-launch team and others from the system schedule interviews with key stakeholders to uncover their concerns, suggestions, and so on. Stakeholder expectations, issues, and suggestions can also be identified by interviewing experts who know and understand what stakeholders expect.

A very powerful and easy-to-manage process for identifying and collecting stakeholder expectations, issues, and suggestions is the Community Engagement Conference which is a very powerful tool in the KWS toolkit. The Community Engagement Conference is designed using Owen's Open Space Technology process (2008). First, a theme for the conference is selected. Then, the pre-launch team identifies key stakeholders and invites them to attend the conference, which can be organized as a half-day, full-day, two-day, or three-day event.

Stakeholders attending the conference are invited to lead small group discussions on topics of interest to them that are related to the theme of the conference. Others who do not want to lead discussions then choose which discussion groups they want to join. Each discussion leader records key points, concerns, issues, and so on, and these are submitted to school system staff in the room who have laptop computers. The notes are then entered into a computer database. At the end of the event the pre-launch team compiles all the notes into one document that is full of stakeholder data that will be used later in the KWS process.

The pre-launch team also conducts a political assessment of the key stakeholders using a stakeholder analysis process like the one described in a World Bank document (online, date unknown) where the stakeholder analysis was described as

> a methodology used to facilitate institutional and policy reform processes by accounting for and often incorporating the needs of those who have a "stake" or an interest in the reforms under consideration. With information on stakeholders, their interests, and their capacity to oppose reform, reform advocates can choose how to best accommodate them, thus assuring policies adopted are politically realistic and sustainable.

The pre-launch team reviews the data collected through their interviews of key stakeholders and from participants in the Community Engagement Conference. They reach consensus on the levels of importance of the stakeholders' key issues, concerns, ideas, and so on; for example, using a Likert-type scale of 1 to 5, where 1 represents very low importance and 5 represents very high importance. Next, they reach consensus on the level of influence (i.e., the power to influence the system's performance) that each key stakeholder has. A Likert-type scale can also be used for this assessment.

The levels of importance and influence create four categories of stakeholders:

1. Those with important issues and a high level of influence.
2. Those with important issues but with a low level of influence.
3. Those with unimportant issues but with a high level of influence.
4. Those with unimportant issues and a low level of influence.

It is reasonable to suggest that the stakeholders in categories 1 and 2 above should be the ones who become the top priority for addressing their issues, concerns, and suggestions. Although categories 1 and 2 represent top priorities, the pre-launch team should not ignore those stakeholders with unimportant issues or low levels of influence. The way in which the pre-launch team responds to those people and their concerns will be observed by others and judgments will be made about how the system treats its stakeholders.

All large-scale change generates political behavior. Some of those behaviors will support school system transformation and others will oppose it.

Table 4.2 Charting Political Constituencies

High Agreement	Bedfellows		Allies
		Fence-sitters	
Low Agreement	Adversaries		Opponents
	Low Trust	High Trust	

A political assessment is conducted using the data collected from the assessments described above, especially from the stakeholder analysis. To conduct the political analysis the pre-launch team can use a strategy developed by Block (1991). Block identified five political constituencies that can emerge during times of change. To identify the constituencies he created a two-dimension chart: a vertical dimension ranging from high agreement with change goals to low agreement with the goals and a horizontal dimension ranging from low trust to high trust. The intersection of the two dimensions created four political groups with a fifth group straddling the middle of the chart. An example of this kind of chart is shown in table 4.2.

1. *Bedfellows*. Bedfellows are fair-weather friends. They support the transformation goals but are not to be trusted because they are fickle and their support can disappear.
2. *Allies*. Allies support the change goals and they are highly trusted to maintain their support. Strong allies are needed to move forward with a transformation journey.
3. *Adversaries*. These people are opposed to the transformation goals and there is a low level of trust. There may be nothing that can be done to convert them into allies.
4. *Opponents*. These are people who are highly trusted, but they disagree with the transformation goals. There is a relatively good chance of converting opponents to allies if their issues are listened to and if adjustments are made to the goals.
5. *Fence-Sitters*. These people cannot decide if they support the transformation goals or not. They prefer to wait and see what others are doing and to gauge how the transformation process is progressing. In the research on the diffusion of innovations they are called the "late majority" and "laggards" (Rogers, 1962). Converting them to allies will be influenced by the success of the transformation journey. Early success will motivate the fence-sitters to support the transformation.

Next, it is possible to merge the levels of importance and influence estimates with the political group assignments as shown in table 4.3. For example, the

Table 4.3 Political Assessment Matrix

	Allies	Bedfellows	Opponents	Adversaries	Fence-sitters
Priority 1 Important issues + high influence					
Priority 2 Important issues + low influence					
Priority 3 Unimportant issues + high influence					
Priority 4 Unimportant issues + low influence					

allies with important issues and with high levels of influence would be posted in the cell for that category; the opponents with unimportant issues but with a high level of influence would be posted in the cell for that category. Given the stakeholders' issues and levels of influence combined with the political group assignments, change-leaders would then make specific decisions about which issues they would respond to. Selection criteria such as the ones listed below could be used to make those decisions (these criteria are only examples—each school system adopting the KWS model would create selection criteria to fit their situation):

- those issues that if addressed could create rapid and significant change (these are called high-leverage changes—those changes that quickly create a cascade of subsequent changes);
- tose issues that if addressed could create early success which would then have a positive effect on the pace of the transformation journey;
- those issues which should be addressed immediately;
- Those issues that should be addressed later; and
- Those issues that should never be addressed.

Finally, using all of the above political assessment data, the pre-launch team completes a force field analysis (Lewin, 1943). The force field analysis identifies forces in support of the proposed transformation and forces opposed to it. If the results indicate that there are more forces opposing the transformation of the district than those in support of it then change-leaders have three possible decisions to make: (1) forget about it, (2) jump in and do it anyway, regardless of the opposition, or (3) postpone starting the transformation while simultaneously conducting activities to reduce opposing forces.

If change-leaders really believe in the need to transform their district then it is obvious that they can't forget about doing it. The second decision above generates a lot of ill will, hurt feelings, political backlash, and ultimate failure of the effort. Thus, the most reasonable decision is to postpone the transformation until there is sufficient political support to begin the journey.

According to Lewin, the third possible decision mentioned above (postpone while working to reduce opposition) can only be effective if change-leaders focus on reducing the opposing forces while maintaining, not increasing, supporting forces. Here is a short anecdote to illustrate the importance of this principle:

> Several years ago the author was chairman of a university committee established to redesign the faculty governance system of the university. An informal force field analysis indicated that one of the strongest supporters of the change was the president of the university. So, the committee attempted to reduce faculty resistance to the changes by touting the president's support, that is, they were trying to increase one of the significant supporting forces. Well, to make a long story short, because the faculty didn't trust the president's motivation for the proposed changes, their resistance increased. The committee had to abandon its tactic quickly. Luckily, the quick switch from playing-up the president's support to playing-down the president's support worked and the governance system was totally redesigned. (Lewin, 1943, pp. 292–310)

The point of the story is not that supporting forces are unimportant—they are very important. But, if change-leaders try to play up the supporting forces they risk increasing resistance to change. Instead, Lewin suggested that change-leaders focus on reducing opposing forces while simultaneously maintaining supporting forces.

There are several ways to reduce opposing forces. One technique is to educate all stakeholders about the need to transform a district. The "educational" activities should be designed carefully. These activities shouldn't be proselytizing sessions or condescending lectures. The activities should present rational and emotional reasons for transforming a school district. Opportunities for group discussion are also provided following a format such as the one suggested Kegan and Laskow Lahey (2002).

Here are a few principles to consider when designing educational activities to reduce opposing forces within a school system (the Community Engagement Conference described earlier can be used to reduce opposing forces in the external environment):

- Conduct an "all-hands" meeting to talk about the proposed transformation. By "all hands," I really mean everybody—teachers, secretaries, janitors, cooks, tutors, specialists, teacher-aides, and so forth). Don't leave anybody out!

Step 1: Pre-Launch Preparation

- If all district employees cannot fit into one conference room, then conduct several all-hands meetings simultaneously in separate locations using distance-learning technologies.
- Another way to get the whole system in the room is to use a sampling technique whereby a "diagonal slice" of the organization is taken to ensure that the "whole system" is represented at the all-hands meeting.

The political assessment process described above is a very important tool because the pre-launch team will need political support to engage a system in a successful transformation journey. The level of political support needed is called the "critical mass." The critical mass of support for an organization change effort consists of the key individuals and a percentage of stakeholders (usually 20–30 percent) who must strongly support the transformation journey if the change is to be implemented successfully (United Nations Institute for Training and Research, date unknown).

The process described above to assess external political support is then repeated but with a focus on building internal political support for the transformation journey. The issues, concerns, and suggestions of teachers, administrators, and support staff are identified. The importance of their issues and their level of influence on the performance of the system are assessed. Internal bedfellows, allies, opponents, adversaries, and fence-sitters are also identified. Communication strategies are devised to work with these political groups.

IDENTIFYING SOURCES OF FINANCIAL RESOURCES

The next activity focuses on identifying where the school system can find financial resources to support the transformation journey. Some strategies for funding transformational change are found in Duffy, Cascarino, and Hensen (2003). At this point in the transformation journey the pre-launch team does not try to appropriate funds—they only identify where they can go to find the money they will need. The main reason for not seeking the funds at this time is that the pre-launch team does not yet have any idea of how much money they will need. An estimate of costs comes later in the KWS process.

READINESS ASSESSMENT

Before making a decision to launch a transformation journey for their school system the pre-launch team assesses their system's readiness to engage in this kind of change using all of the data they collected during the pre-launch preparation phase. This assessment is absolutely critical for the future success of the transformation effort. One example of a readiness assessment instrument was created by the Information Technology Leadership Academy (2014) for the state of California. This tool assesses a system's readiness based on communication processes, level of internal sponsorship for the change, level of stakeholder support for the change, level of the system's capacity to change (resources, knowledge, and skills), and availability of training opportunities.

MAKE A LAUNCH/DON'T LAUNCH DECISION

Given all of the data collected using the tools and processes described above, the pre-launch team makes a "launch/don't launch" decision. The "launch" decision would initiate a deeper and broader transformation effort. The "don't launch" decision would stop the process until an acceptable level of system readiness for change is reached, or it would terminate the transformation journey.

If the decision is to launch a full-blown transformation then the pre-launch team forms and trains an SLT and appoints and trains one or more Knowledge Work Supervisors (school systems adopting KWS are advised to invent a name for these supervisors that fits their situation). Role descriptions for the SLT and the Knowledge Work Supervisors were presented in chapter 5. Change-leadership standards and proposed certification standards for Knowledge Work Supervisors are found in volume 2 of this book along with a description of a design for a preparation program to train educators to serve as Knowledge Work Supervisors.

At the end of KWS Step 1, a school system is now ready to make a transition into KWS Step 2. Activities, tasks, and processes for the redesign phase are described in the next chapter.

REFERENCES

Block, P. (1991). *The empowered manager: Positive political skills at work.* San Francisco: Berrett-Koehler.

Duffy, F. M., Cascarino, J. and Henson, C. (2003). Financing systemic transformational change–where can you find the money? Retrieved on January 11, 2016, from: http://www.futureminds.us/document/Financing%20Systemic%20Change.pdf.

Kegan, R. and Laskow Lahey, L. (2002). *How the way we talk can change the way we work: Seven languages for transformation.* San Francisco: Jossey-Bass.

Information Technology Leadership Academy (2014). Organizational change management readiness guide. Sacramento, CA: California State Government. Retrieved on January 10, 2016, from: http://www.cio.ca.gov/opd/pdf/itla/21/OCM-FISCal-Readiness-Guide.pdf.

Lewin, K. (1943, May). Defining the field at a .given time. *Psychological Review* *50*(3): 292–310, DOI: 10.1037/h0062738.

Owen, H. (2008). *Open Space Technology: A user's guide* (3rd ed.). San Francisco, CA: Berrett-Koehler.

Rogers, E. (1962). *Diffusion of innovations* (1st ed.). New York, NY: Free Press.

United Nations Institute for Training and Research (date unknown). Developing a "Critical Mass" of Support for the Change. Accessed on May 2, 2016 from: http://www.unitar.org/hiroshima/sites/unitar.org.hiroshima/files/17_AF07WSI_Developing_Critical_Mass.pdf.

World Bank Group (date unknown). Stakeholder analysis. Retrieved on January 10, 2016, from: http://www1.worldbank.org/publicsector/anticorrupt/PoliticalEconomy/PDFVersion.pdf.

Chapter Five

Step 2: Redesign the Entire System

America's school systems, for the most part, are designed to comply with the requirements of the Industrial Age. Because of this design, it is not surprising for some educators and noneducators to know that the relationships that school systems have with their external environments, their core and support work processes, and the design of their internal social infrastructures are outmoded and ill-suited to the demands of our Knowledge-Age society. While most of our nation's organizations have made or are making the transition to Knowledge Age organization designs and processes, most school systems are not making that journey.

In many of our school systems, the relationships they have with the external environment can be characterized as crisis management. "Outsiders" are sometimes viewed as intruders and potentially threatening to the system. Top school administrators find themselves in combative relationships with their school boards, parent groups, and their communities. The needs, concerns, and issues held by key stakeholders in the environment are discounted as irrelevant or "crazy." As a result of the ineffective relationships, the school system becomes a fortress that strives to protect the status quo while fighting the fires of change that are ignited by the external stakeholders.

The Industrial-Age patterns of organizing the core and support work of school systems (i.e., teaching, learning, and administrative supports) have become so ingrained that despite the known shortcomings of these patterns it is extraordinarily difficult for educators to imagine how to do their work differently. The core and support work processes are often fragmented and managed piecemeal. The inability or unwillingness to manage the work processes as a whole prevents educators from providing children with a quality education that prepares them for success in our twenty-first-century society.

Many of us who write about, teach, and present on how to create and sustain transformational change in school systems (see Reigeluth & Karnopp, 2013) believe that it is inappropriate and ineffective to tinker with the pieces of the work processes while assuming that the tinkering will create significant change and improvements. Principles of whole-system change must be applied if significant improvements are desired because the core and support work processes are actually subsystems of a larger school system.

The quality of work life for educators can be demotivating and dissatisfying. The quality of work life is significantly affected by the design of a school system's internal social infrastructure. The social infrastructure is composed of leadership behavior, organization culture, organization design, the reward system, the dominant mental model held by the system (reflected in the mission and vision statements), and communication processes, among others. Ideally, the social infrastructure supports people as they do their work by removing system-based obstacles that prevent educators from working at a high level of performance.

Given the issues identified above with the relationships that school systems have with their environments, the outmoded core and support work processes, and the demotivating quality of work life, I believe that entire school systems must be transformed along three paths:

Path 1: Transform the environmental relationships.
Path 2: Transform the core and support work processes.
Path 3: Transform the internal social infrastructure.

Further, I believe that a transformed instructional supervision process could be the ideal process for transforming school systems along those three paths. The name of the transformed instructional supervision process that I support is Knowledge Work Supervision (KWS), which is the focus of this book. From this point forward, I will offer some practical advice about how to create change along the three paths using the KWS methodology.

STEP 2: REDESIGN THE ENTIRE SYSTEM

Near the end of Step 1: Pre-Launch Preparation, after a Strategic Leadership Team (SLT) and a Knowledge Work Supervisor have been identified and trained, the school system then makes a transition to Step 2 of the KWS process. Step 2 is complex and will require significant time and resources to complete successfully; complex, however, doesn't mean impossible—it only means there is a lot to accomplish.

Step 2: Redesign the Entire System

Step 2 begins as the SLT organizes their system into academic and support work clusters; for example, an academic cluster could be a single high school and all the middle and elementary schools that feed into it and a support work cluster could be the central administration office. Then, each cluster creates a Cluster Redesign Team (CRT) to manage the transformation process within the cluster. The CRTs receive training on principles of systemic change.

Next, the SLT identifies a single academic cluster that they believe has the potential to succeed in the early stages of the transformation journey. The academic cluster selected to start the transformation process should not be the highest-performing one in the system nor should it be the lowest-performing one. It should be an average performing cluster with the potential to succeed with their transformation. The "not the best/not the worst" strategy requires an explanation. According to Pasmore (1988, 1992), if a high-performing work unit is selected to start the transformation and if they succeed, then people in other parts of the organization will say something like "they had all the best people" or "they had the most resources." If a low-performing cluster is selected, it will almost certainly fail because it doesn't have the capacity to engage successfully in the transformation process.

The SLT also notifies the central administration cluster that it will be starting its transformation journey at the same time as the first academic cluster. Transforming the central administration cluster early in the KWS process is very important because that collection of support functions has significant and substantial control of resources needed by the first academic cluster to begin the transformation journey. Also, the hierarchical and bureaucratic culture often found in central administration offices is diametrically opposed to the democratic principles underpinning the KWS process.

With the academic and support work clusters formed and the CRTs in place and trained, KWS begins with a System Engagement Conference. This conference is designed using Weisbord and Janoff's (1995) "Future Search" methodology. Because the System Engagement Conference requires participants to engage over a three-day period, it is likely that the System Engagement Conference will need to be convened over the summer months. Financial resources may be needed to help faculty and staff to participate.

The System Engagement Conference is a three-day planning meeting that enables participants to arrive at a consensus about a desirable future for their school system. It is also an ideal process for dealing with complex situations, including those of high conflict and uncertainty. The System Engagement Conference brings into one room those with resources, expertise, formal authority, and need. Participants meet for sixteen hours spread across three days. The meeting design comes from theories and principles tested in many cultures for the past half-century. It relies on mutual learning among participants as a catalyst for voluntary action and follow-up. There are specific conditions that must be met if the conference is to be successful. These conditions are (Future Search Network, online)

- Get the "whole system" in the room. This condition doesn't mean that 100 percent of the district's faculty and staff are in one room. What it means is that each part of a school system must be represented in the conference. This condition is met by inviting a carefully selected cross-section of faculty and staff who have a stake in the district's mission, vision, and outcomes.
- Explore the whole system before seeking to fix any part. Get everyone talking about the same system.
- Seek common ground and focus on the future. Don't engage in problem-solving or conflict resolution. Acknowledge the problems and conflicts as "information" and then move on.
- Encourage self-management and responsibility for action by participants throughout the conference.
- Urge full attendance—do not permit part-time participation.
- Ensure that the conference room provides participants with a relaxed and healthy environment (e.g., comfortable chairs, rooms with windows, appropriate heat or air conditioning, healthy snacks and meals, and adequate breaks).
- Ensure that the conference is scheduled across three days. Encourage participants to reflect on conference outcomes after leaving at the end of each day (this kind of reflection is called "soak time").
- Make sure you get a public commitment to support the ongoing transformation journey before the conference adjourns.

The System Engagement Conference is organized as follows:

- Day 1: Afternoon session
  1. *Focus on the past.* Small groups construct timelines of key events in the history of their school system. Group participants tell stories about the system's history and discuss the implications of that history for their system's transformation journey.
  2. *Focus on present, external trends.* The whole group makes a "mind map" of external environmental trends affecting their system and identifies the most important trends that will likely affect their system.

- Day 2: Morning session
  1. *Focus on present, external trends.* Small groups describe how the external trends, identified in activity 2 above, are currently being handled, and they discuss how they want to handle these trends in the future.

2. *Focus on the present.* Small groups discuss their school system's current performance and identify what they are proud of and what disappoints them about the system's performance.

- Day 2: Afternoon session
    1. *Describe ideal future scenarios.* Small groups imagine their system in the future and they describe their preferred future for their school system as if it has already been accomplished.
    2. *Identify common ground.* The preferred futures are described, and small groups identify themes that are woven through all of the scenarios. This activity stakes out common ground for all the participants.

- Day 3: Morning and early afternoon sessions
    1. *Confirm common ground.* The whole group engages in dialogue to seek and agree upon a shared vision for the future of their system.
    2. *Action planning.* Volunteers sign up to create action plans to move forward with the transformation journey.

The primary outcomes of the System Engagement Conference are a "fuzzy vision" for a desirable future for the district, the recalibration of the district's strategic direction, identification of the boundaries within which change activities will be permissible or impermissible (the SLT may need to negotiate with their state department of education to get waiver from state education requirements), and action plans for the first two clusters to begin the transformation journey (the first academic cluster and the central administration cluster).

The term *fuzzy vision*, above, requires an explanation. In the field of organization change, there is a principle called "minimal critical specification" (Cummings & Worley, 2013) or minimal specificity. In practical terms this principle means that the envisioned change should not be overly specific. It should be specific enough to allow educators to know where the system wants to go but not so specific that educators who didn't participate in the System Engagement Conference cannot add to it.

A simple analogy that I use to help people understand the principle of minimal specificity for creating vision statements is a paint-by-number canvas. The canvas has a figure on it in outline form. When looking at the canvas, it is not necessary to "imagine" what the image is because there is just enough specificity to see it. Then, as colors are added, a beautiful picture emerges. In the same way, a system's new fuzzy vision should be like a paint-by-number canvas with just enough detail to help educators recognize the future system that is envisioned. Educators working in the system then start creating transformational change by embellishing the vision by filling in new details.

Giving people the chance to add to the vision is important because people tend to support what they help create (Karlin, 2007).

Another important outcome of the System Engagement Conference is that faculty and staff will know and understand that transforming their system will require simultaneous change along three paths:

1. Path 1: Transform environmental relationships.
2. Path 2: Transform core and support work processes.
3. Path 3: Transform internal social infrastructure.

Sometimes people see this three-path metaphor and assume that it is a sequential, step-by-step change process. It is not. Change created along these paths must be simultaneous. Change-leaders cannot first change environmental relationships, then change core and support work processes, and then change the internal social infrastructure.

The reason for simultaneous change is that these three pathways are intertwined and changes along one path require complementary changes in the others; for example, if change-leaders want to transform their system, they need positive and strong relationships with key stakeholders in the external environment. To get that kind of support, change-leaders need to have great ideas for improving teaching, learning, and support services. And, if change-leaders make changes to the core and support work processes they also need to make complementary changes to the social infrastructure.

Failure to conceive of the change process as a set of three simultaneous change-paths increases the likelihood of being unable to sustain the changes that are being made because the three sets of changes must be interrelated and complementary. So, as plans are made to transform the system in the System Engagement Conference, the participants must subscribe to the principle of simultaneous change.

Following the System Engagement Conference, the first two CRTs (the first academic cluster and the central office cluster) organize redesign workshops for their faculty and staff. The redesign workshops are three-day events designed using the "participative design" principles described by Emery (1993). More than one may be required. The redesign workshops are organized as follows:

- Selected educators and staff from each cluster participate. It is important to select participants who support the transformation journey and have the knowledge, skills, and motivation to make the journey successful.
- Participants engage in specific activities (described later in this chapter) to create ideas for redesigning the cluster's environmental relationships (both clusters focus on their relationship with other parts of the school system;

the central office cluster also focuses on the relationship of the entire system with its external environment), core and support work processes, and internal social infrastructure.
- The CRTs gather all the ideas for change that were proposed. The CRTs identify ideas to include in a comprehensive proposal to redesign their clusters. The ideas selected for the proposal must comply with the parameters created in the System Engagement Conference that identified permissible and impermissible changes.
- The CRT submits their comprehensive proposal to the SLT for review and approval.
- Changes to the proposal by the SLT must be negotiated with the CRT.
- The SLT reviews the final proposal and estimates required resources.
- The SLT submits the final proposal and cost estimates to the school board and perhaps to their state department of education.
- Start-up funds to implement each cluster's change proposal are provided while seeking additional funds to continue the clusters' transformation.
- The CRTs then launch the transformation journey within their clusters.

As each cluster engages in transformation activities, they also engage in formative evaluation of their process and its outcomes. The methodology used for formative evaluation is called "On-Track Seminars," which are designed using principles of Preskill and Torres' (1999) evaluative inquiry. The outcomes of these seminars are used to keep the transformation journey on the right course toward the system's desirable future—the desirable future that was envisioned in the System Engagement Conference.

While the first two clusters are engaging in transformational change, the remaining clusters in the school district are taking steps to learn how they can effectively engage in transformational change when their turn comes. Their learning is guided by principles of organization learning (Argyris & Schön, 1978; Fulmer, Gibbs & Keys, 1998).

One goal of KWS is for the school system to become a knowledge-creating organization. This happens as system-wide experience, knowledge, and skills learned by the first two clusters that began the transformation journey are disseminated to other clusters. The dissemination occurs by asking members of the first two clusters to become mentors and trainers for the remaining CRTs. Further, the Knowledge Work Supervisor collaborates with the CRTs to ensure that their process and outcomes comply with the redesign parameters created in the earlier System Engagement Conference.

After the system and all of its clusters are transformed, the SLT and Knowledge Work Supervisor evaluate the transformation process and outcomes. The evaluation methodology that I recommend is Stufflebeam's Context Inputs Process Product (CIPP) methodology (2007). This methodology, and the On-Track Seminar method mentioned earlier, will be described in more detail in chapter 9.

Up to this point, I have outlined the general features of KWS Step 2. Step 2 begins with the SLT organizing their school system into clusters; continues with a System Engagement Conference that creates a fuzzy vision of a desirable future for their system and generates a set of parameters that defines changes that are permissible and impermissible; empowers the first two clusters to begin the transformation journey; organizes redesign workshops within the first two clusters that result in specific change ideas to redesign the clusters' environmental relationships, core and support work processes, and internal social infrastructure; and engages all remaining clusters in transformational change.

Clearly, Step 2 is complex and it will require time to complete. Pasmore (1988, 1992) suggested that a total system redesign effort can take anywhere from eighteen to thirty-six months for a small organization and five to seven years for larger organizations.

Now, let's take a closer look at what happens in the redesign workshops by focusing on the three change-paths that must be followed to create transformational change.

PATH 1: TRANSFORM ENVIRONMENTAL RELATIONSHIPS

All the data from the pre-launch preparation phase are fed into the System Engagement Conference that is scheduled early in Step 2 of KWS. Conference participants analyze the data to redefine their system's mission and vision and to set a new strategic direction for their system. They also use the data to create plans to implement the transformation journey throughout their system.

The core strategy for implementing the transformation plan is to empower the first academic cluster and its component schools and the central administration cluster to engage in transformational change activities that help them (1) transform the clusters' environmental relationships, core and support work processes, and internal social infrastructure; (2) propose changes that are aligned with the district's new mission, vision, and strategic direction; and (3) propose changes that make sense for their cluster.

The External Environment

A school district is a system. All systems exist within an external environment. School systems have an open relationship with their environments because they require human, financial, and technical resources from the environment to achieve their goals. They also require political support to create and sustain change. The academic and support work clusters within a school system also exist within a broader environment; that is, the school system itself is the external environment for each cluster. The quality of the relationships with the external environment is very important because the whole system and its clusters require resources that the environment provides. The external environment for individual clusters and schools is the larger school system within which they are situated. The larger system provides the clusters and schools with the resources they need to function effectively.

The redesign of environmental relationships begins in KWS Step 1 (see chapter 6). During the early stages of the pre-launch preparation phase, a small leadership team composed of the superintendent and a few trusted colleagues explore the possibility of taking their school system on a transformation journey. As part of this exploration they confer with carefully selected key external and internal stakeholders, including state department of education representatives, to get a sense of the level of political support for the transformation. They also scan the environment for potential threats that could disrupt their transformation journey and to identify opportunities that could be seized for the benefit of the system.

Later in the pre-launch phase, carefully selected external stakeholders are invited to participate in a Community Engagement Conference where participants self-organize into small discussion groups. The discussions focus on topics of interest to the participants as they relate to the future of the school system. Key discussion points are recorded and submitted to a central location in the conference room where they are entered into a computer database.

A political assessment of key stakeholders is also conducted during the pre-launch phase. The level of importance of key stakeholders' issues and their level of influence on the system are estimated. The key stakeholders' level of agreement with the transformation journey and the level of trust that the pre-launch team has in those stakeholders are also estimated, resulting in the stakeholders being identified as allies, bedfellows, opponents, adversaries, or fence-sitters.

Participants in the System Engagement Conference analyze and discuss the environmental assessment data. They then summarize what they learned from the analysis and create broadly defined criteria for redesigning environmental relationships by using the major learning from the environmental analysis.

Each school system engaged in KWS will have different environmental relationships that will require unique responses to improve those relationships. Thus, it is impossible for me to provide a definitive list of possible ways to improve those relationships. However, I can recommend one process that can be used by all school systems to improve their environmental relationships. It's called strategic communication (Duffy & Chance, 2007).

Strategic communication is a process used to influence stakeholders' behavior to gain support for a school system's transformation journey. The process answers three core questions: (1) With whom do you need to communicate? (2) What message(s) need to be communicated? and (3) How will you communicate these messages? The strategic communications methodology flows like this:

1. Analyze the situation (during pre-launch preparation) by conducting an environmental scan.
2. Identify key stakeholders' issues, concerns, and ideas and estimate the relative importance of their issues and their level of influence on system performance. Also, estimate the political group to which each of the key stakeholders belongs: allies, bedfellows, opponents, adversaries, or fence-sitters.
3. Set objectives to be accomplished through strategic communication.
4. Devise communication strategies for each of the political groups listed above.
5. Create tactics and activities for each communication strategy.
6. Implement the strategic communication plan.
7. Evaluate the outcomes.

Please don't forget that each academic and support work unit cluster will be also be using strategic communication to improve their relationships with other parts of the school system.

PATH 2: TRANSFORM CORE AND SUPPORT WORK PROCESSES

In KWS Step 1, the SLT organized their system into academic and support work clusters. Then, at the beginning of KWS Step 2, they conducted a System Engagement Conference that resulted in a redefined mission, vision, and strategic direction for the entire system. Next, they empowered and enabled an average performing academic cluster and the central administration cluster to begin their system's transformation journey and formed a CRT for each cluster. Later in Step 2, the CRTs organized Cluster Engagement Conferences to engage educators and staff within their clusters in the transformation process.

In the Cluster Engagement Conferences, participants analyzed their core and support work processes to identify how those processes could be transformed. There are two strategies that can be used to do these analyses. The first goes by the name "business process reengineering" (Hammer & Champy, 1993). The second is called "paradigm shifting."

Reengineering

A key reengineering principle is the clean slate approach to redesigning work processes. This principle says that when it comes to organizational redesign, nothing is sacred—everything is subject to reengineering. However, reengineering seems to examine only the work processes of an organization. It does not try to "reengineer" the social infrastructure. I regard this model as flawed because the work processes and the social infrastructure must be redesigned and improved simultaneously (Pasmore, 1988; Pava, 1983). Nevertheless, I believe the process can be modified and used to analyze the traditional linear instructional program in a school system (i.e., often organized as prekindergarten through twelfth grade) and the system's internal social infrastructure (discussed later in the chapter) (Duffy, 1996).

To use reengineering principles effectively the entire linear instructional program (e.g., pre-K–12th grade) must be examined and transformed, not just parts of it (e.g., not just the middle school, not just the language arts curriculum, or not just the high school). One of the reasons the entire work process must be improved is because of a systems change principle expressed as "upstream errors flow downstream" (Pasmore, 1988).

The "upstream errors flow downstream" principle reflects the fact that mistakes made early in a work process flow downstream, are compounded, and create more problems later on in the process. An example of this principle in action is found in the research on high school dropouts. Research suggests that most future dropouts may be identified as early as sixth grade and many can be identified even earlier. A study by Balfanz and Herzog (2005) indicated that more than half of sixth graders with the following three criteria eventually left school: attend school less than 80 percent of the time, receive a low final grade from their teachers in behavior, and fail either math or English. These upstream errors (low student attendance, low grades, failing math or English) flow downstream and result in high school dropouts.

Paradigm Shifting

The reengineering approach to redesigning core and support work processes does not create new ways to teach and learn. Reengineering preserves the Industrial Age linear instructional program while making changes within that program. There is another approach to redesigning that can result in what is known as paradigm shifting. Many change-minded educators (Duffy, 2011; McCombs, 2008; Reigeluth, 2013; and Reigeluth & Karnopp, 2013) believe that teaching and learning must shift from traditional classroom teaching to "learner-centered education" which could include some of the following characteristics:

- personalized, self-directed learning;
- project and problem-based activities;
- flexible blocks of study and activity times;
- multidisciplinary curricula with team teaching;
- teachers as mentors and facilitators;
- technologies used as essential resources for teaching and learning; and
- performance-based assessment of student learning with mastery as the goal.

Changes in classroom teaching and learning as suggested above require systematic planning for instructional design, new teaching and learning methods, innovative strategies for assessing student learning, and new metrics for measuring program success (Reigeluth, 2013).

Although reengineering the instructional program or creating a paradigm shift to improve student learning is an important goal for redesigning the core and support work processes of a school district, focusing only on improving student learning is a piecemeal approach to improvement. A teacher's knowledge and literacy is probably one of the more important factors influencing student learning (see Sanders & Rivers, 1996). So, taking steps to enhance the professional intellect of teachers using KWS should also be part of any school district's transformation efforts. Principles for enhancing the professional intellect of teachers are simple, yet powerful (adapted from Pava, 1983):

- Improve the quality and timeliness of key information that teachers and support staff need to be effective.
- Ensure that teachers and support staff interact with the key people who have the critical information they need to be effective.
- Provide teachers and support staff with a variety of structured, semistructured, and informal forums for exchanging information (e.g., in structured communities of practice, workshops, informal "brown bag" lunches, or national conferences).
- Examine and improve any devices (e.g., computers), work procedures (e.g., lesson planning), and organizational functions (e.g., administration and supervision) that support teaching (i.e., improve the support work processes and devices).

Quinn, Anderson, and Finkelstein (1996) offered additional strategies that can be used to enhance professional intellect. Their strategies were adapted for KWS:

- Recruit the best applicants to fill positions, where best means those with highly desirable and proven knowledge, skills, and dispositions.
- Require participation in intensive early professional development activities.

- Increase professional challenges by using job enrichment strategies.
- Evaluate job performance and remove low performers.
- Boost professionals' problem-solving abilities by creating an organization-wide knowledge management system that they can access.
- Overcome professionals' reluctance to share information by creating communities of practice and require participants to share their learning.
- Organize the system around professional intellect by empowering and enabling faculty and staff to create customized solutions to problems they experience at work.
- Invert the system's organization design by putting faculty and staff at the top of the organization chart and senior administrators and other support personnel below them on the chart.
- Create intellectual webs by encouraging and supporting the formation of self-organizing communities of practice staffed by like-minded people who share a common interest or work task.

Further, while improving student and teacher learning are two important goals of transforming core and support work processes in a school district, this is also a piecemeal approach to transforming a school district because that system is a knowledge-creating organization and it is, or should be, a learning organization. Professional knowledge must be created and embedded in a school district's operational structures, and organizational learning must occur if a school district wants to develop and maintain the capacity to provide children with a quality education. So, school system learning (i.e., organizational learning through KWS) must also be part of a district's transformation strategy.

An example of one process for transforming a school system into a knowledge-creating organization is provided by Nonaka and Takeuchi (1995). They called their approach "hypertext." They summarized that approach as follows:

> As knowledge and innovation become more central to competitive success, it should come as no surprise that there has been growing dissatisfaction with traditional organizational structures. For most of this century, organizational structure has oscillated between two basic types: bureaucracy and task force. But when it comes to knowledge creation, neither of these structures is adequate. What is necessary is some combination or synthesis of the two. (Nonaka & Takeuchi, 1995, p. 160)

The hypertext design provides knowledge-creating organizations with the " strategic ability to acquire, create, exploit, and accumulate new knowledge continuously and repeatedly in a cyclical process" (Nonaka & Takeuchi, 1995, p. 166). Nonaka and Takeuchi's approach if used as part of the KWS protocol may offer school districts—which are knowledge-creating organizations—a new organization design that supports their desire to become high-performing knowledge-creating systems.

Lipnack and Stamps (1993) offered another innovative approach to designing knowledge organizations. Their approach is called "Teamnet." "Teamnets" are networks of teams that cross traditional boundaries, such as departmental, divisional, or functional boundaries. Lipnack and Stamps described the "Five Teamnet Principles" (p. 30). They are as follows:

- Teams must have a clear purpose.
- They must be composed of independent members who want to work together.
- Ongoing interaction is needed among team members.
- Two or more leaders are required.
- Teams must have connections to different levels of the existing hierarchy.

Core work is maintained and enriched by support work. In school districts, support work roles include all roles in the central office, instructional technologists, building principals, supervisors, education specialists, librarians, cafeteria workers, janitors, bus drivers, and others. Support work is important to the success of a school district, but it is not the most important work. Classroom teaching and learning is the most important work and it must be elevated to that status if a school system wants to increase its overall effectiveness.

Clearly, transforming core and support work processes requires some deep thinking about which redesign approach to use: reengineering or paradigm shifting. Change-leaders must also remember that teachers are knowledge workers and their school systems are knowledge-creating organizations. Redesigning a school system based on those realities also requires innovative thinking to devise specific change strategies. This deep and innovative thinking begins in the System Engagement Conference in the early phases of KWS Step 2 and then continues within the academic and central administration clusters targeted to start the transformation journey.

PATH 3: REDESIGN THE INTERNAL SOCIAL INFRASTRUCTURE

Social Infrastructure

In the sociotechnical systems design literature, social infrastructure is referred to as the social system. I use the term "social infrastructure" instead because I think it is a better description of the form and shape of the social system. Social infrastructure is an element of organization design that gives order, balance, and unity to the work processes of the organization. The social infrastructure also supports and maintains the work processes. It is the element that relates all parts of the organization to each other and to the whole. In this respect, assessing and improving the social infrastructure is a critical part of organizational reengineering or paradigm shifting. Yet, it is also an often overlooked part of organizational improvement (except in organizational improvement models based on sociotechnical systems theory). Although making improvements to the social infrastructure is often overlooked, the sociotechnical systems literature says very clearly that for true, long-lasting organizational improvement to occur, the core and support work processes and social infrastructure must be "jointly optimized" (Pasmore, 1988), not one improved at the expense of the other.

The social infrastructure is composed of the roles and relationships professionals need to establish and maintain to get the work done, the critical job skills needed to do the work, human motivation and job satisfaction (quality of work life variables), and organization design, among others. These variables interact to operate and maintain the work processes of the school district. Identifying weaknesses and opportunities in the social infrastructure, and then taking steps to make improvements, increases the likelihood that a transformation journey will succeed and persist.

Roles and Relationships

Role theory provides insights for redesigning organizations for high performance. The part an individual plays in a school district is called a role. "Each role has formal, explicit, job-related requirements and informal, implicit, social requirements" (Van Fleet, Griffin, & Moorhead, 1991, p. 313). People in organizations expect individuals to play a certain part in the organization. The "sent role" is the formal information provided to an individual about his or her role.

The "sent role" is often perceived differently than intended. This is called the perceived role. Thus, the role actually played may be different from the expected role. When these differences are severe, role ambiguity or role conflict may result. Determining essential roles and assessing the degree of similarity between "sent roles" and "perceived roles" and the resultant levels of role ambiguity and role conflict is one of the important diagnoses made during the redesign workshops within the academic and central administration clusters.

Critical Job Skills

Every job requires critical skills to do it effectively and efficiently. Teaching is no different. Robinson and Robinson (1996) provided a means to identify and chart critical job skills. They did this by making a distinction between key requirements (critical skills), basic requirements, and low requirements. Data about these job requirements are collected from "top performers" who know the most about the relative importance of practices and skill levels required for their roles.

Another approach to identifying critical job skills was reported by the American Society for Training and Development (ASTD) (1983). They conducted a competency study to identify and prescribe critical competencies for training and development specialists. Modified for teaching, their process can be used to do the following:

- Determine the domain of teaching by distinguishing it from other roles in schools.
- Determine key roles teachers must play.
- Identify major environmental factors expected to impact teaching in the future.
- Identify the critical outputs expected of teaching.
- Identify critical teaching competencies.
- Develop behavioral anchors for the teaching competencies ("anchors" are behavioral descriptions of what the competencies look like at various levels of expertise).
- Cluster the various teaching roles to reflect common competency requirements.

The ASTD competency model can also be used to identify key competencies for support staff.

Once critical skills are identified, teachers and support staff are engaged in a process of performance consulting. Clinical supervision (Goldhammer, 1969; Cogan, 1973) could continue to be an effective tool in schools as a performance consulting model that helps educators raise their individual skill levels. Goals, strategies, and methods for raising individual levels of performance are created in the cluster-based redesign workshops and included in the comprehensive transformation proposal that each cluster submits to the SLT.

Motivation and Job Satisfaction

Another important part of the analysis of the social infrastructure is the assessment of the degree to which organizational roles stimulate internal motivation in people. The psychological characteristics of a role that contribute to motivation are called motivators. Motivators, in conjunction with satisfiers, influence the quality of work life in organizations. Emery and Thorsrud (1976) called these motivators "psychological criteria for productive work."

Six Psychological Criteria for Productive Work

Part A: Job Content

These job content criteria are rated by faculty and staff in their cluster's redesign workshops. Participants are asked to rate each criterion from −5 (too little) to +5 (too much). A "0" rating represents an ideal amount.

1. *Adequate elbow room*: People feel that they control how they do their work. On the one hand, the boss is not "breathing down their necks;" on the other hand, they have enough discretion to know what to do on their own.
2. *Opportunity to learn*: This involves two distinct elements—
   - Setting goals: People are able to set challenging yet reasonable goals for their work.
   - Getting feedback: People get timely feedback on their progress toward their goals.
3. *Optimal variety*: People have an optimal amount of variety in their work; they are neither bored nor overwhelmed.

Part B: Social Climate of the Workplace

These criteria are rated 0 (none) to 10 (lots). It is impossible to have too much of these in a workplace.

4. *Mutual support and respect*: People get help and support from their coworkers. People cooperate, rather than compete. Individuals' unique capabilities are recognized.
5. *Meaningfulness*: This involves two distinct elements—
   - Social usefulness: People believe that the product or service they produce improves their customers' quality of life or that their work contributes to the general welfare of their society. Their product or service is of high quality and value.
   - Seeing the "whole product": People are able to see the whole product and understand how their work contributes to the end product or service.
6. *Desirable career path*: People see the opportunities to move on to new jobs that provide more opportunities for personal growth and for learning new skills. They do not feel that they are in a "dead-end" job.

Emery and Thorsrud's six psychological criteria represent the key features of an organization design often characterized as participative. The educators and support staff participating in their cluster-based redesign workshops assess the degree to which these psychological criteria exist within their clusters. If specific variables called motivators exist at high levels then their internal social infrastructure is considered to be highly motivating, but if they exist at low levels then the internal social infrastructure is considered to be demotivating.

To measure these criteria, redesign workshop participants assess their internal social infrastructure using the diagnostic matrix shown in table 5.1. Each individual participant makes his or her assessment of the quality of the cluster's internal social infrastructure, and then the individual results are combined into a group diagnostic profile. Redesign workshop participants then create specific ideas for raising the six psychological criteria to optimal levels. By raising each of the six psychological criteria to optimal levels, job satisfaction and motivation should improve. The suggested changes are included in the comprehensive transformation proposal that is submitted to the SLT.

In addition to creating ideas to bring the six psychological criteria to optimal levels within their clusters, the participants examine their reward system to ensure that the changes they will make will be rewarded and reinforced. Assessing the reward system and making necessary changes to it is a critically important step because an organization's reward system is one of the central threats to change as it often does not reinforce desired changes—rather it reinforces the status quo. Further, Thorndike (1905) showed us that behavior that is reinforced is repeated and behavior that is repeated is learned. Reward systems need to be transformed to reinforce desirable new behaviors.

So, in summary, educators and support staff in the redesign workshops can take the following actions to improve motivation and morale in their clusters:

1. Ask individuals to assess the degree to which the six psychological criteria that affect motivation and job satisfaction exist in their work environment.
2. Combine the responses to create a group matrix.
3. Use the group matrix to create ideas to transform their cluster's internal social infrastructure to improve motivation and morale.
4. Retool the reward system to support the desired changes.

Organizational Structure and Design

"Organizational structure is a system of authority, reporting, and task relationships that defines the form and function of the organization's activities. The structure determines how the parts of the organization fit together" (Van

Table 5.1 Psychological Criteria Diagnostic Worksheet

Part A: Job Content

These criteria are rated in specially designed workshops. Employees are asked to rate each criterion from −5 (too little) to +5 (too much). A "0" rating represents an ideal amount.

Adequate Elbow Room: People feel that they control how they do their work. On the one hand, the boss is not "breathing down their necks;" on the other hand, they have enough discretion to know what to do on their own.

Opportunity to Learn: This involves two distinct elements—

Setting goals: People are able to set challenging yet reasonable goals for their work.

Getting feedback: People get timely feedback on their progress toward their goals.

Optimal Variety: People have an optimal amount of variety in their work; they are neither bored nor overwhelmed.

	Too Little	Ideal	Too Much
1. Adequate Elbow Room	−5 −4 −3 −2 −1	0	+1 +2 +3 +4 +5
2. Opportunity to Learn			
Setting goals	−5 −4 −3 −2 −1	0	+1 +2 +3 +4 +5
Getting feedback	−5 −4 −3 −2 −1	0	+1 +2 +3 +4 +5
3. Optimal Variety	−5 −4 −3 −2 −1	0	+1 +2 +3 +4 +5

Part B: Social Climate of the Workplace These criteria are rated "0" (none) to 10 (lots). It is impossible to have too much of these in a workplace.

Mutual Support and Respect: People get help and support from their coworkers. People cooperate, rather than compete. Individuals' unique capabilities are recognized.

Meaningfulness: This involves two distinct elements—

Social usefulness: People believe that the product or service they produce improves their customers' quality of life or that their work contributes to the general welfare of their society. Their product or service is of high quality and value.

Seeing the "whole product": People are able to see the whole product and understand how their work contributes to the end product or service.

Desirable Career Path: People see the opportunities to move on to new jobs that provide more opportunities for personal growth and learning new skills. They do not feel that they are in a "dead-end" job.

	None ⟵⟶ Lots
4. Mutual Support and Respect	0 1 2 3 4 5 6 7 8 9 10
5. Meaningfulness	
Social usefulness	0 1 2 3 4 5 6 7 8 9 10
Seeing the "whole product"	0 1 2 3 4 5 6 7 8 9 10
6. Desirable Career Path	0 1 2 3 4 5 6 7 8 9 10

Fleet, Griffin, & Moorhead, 1991, p. 325). Two key concepts of organizational structure are responsibility and authority. Responsibility is an obligation to do something. Authority is the legitimate right to do it. Other concepts of organizational structure include organizational charts, division of labor, departmentalization, span of control, administrative hierarchy, centralization of decision making, and formalization of rules and procedures. All of these elements of organization design affect individual, team, school, cluster, and system performance.

There are three classic approaches to organizational structure: Weber's "Ideal Bureaucracy" (1947), Fayol's "Principles of Organizing" (1949), and Likert's "Human Organization" (1961). These approaches are anchored to the Industrial Age and persist today. The traditional organization design of school districts fits well with Weber's and Fayol's design principles. However, during the past couple of decades, school districts have experimented with two different organization designs. The first is called "school-based management" and the other is called "charter schools."

Although school-based management (SBM) and charter schools are popular strategies for improving schooling, from a sociotechnical systems perspective, in my opinion, there is a very serious problem with both of these approaches. First, SBM does not support a view of districts as whole-systems composed of individual schools that must be coordinated to achieve desirable educational results for all students. To use a naval metaphor, SBM is like telling each ship in a fleet to make its own way. In real naval fleets, each individual ship is under its own power, but the fleet is coordinated so it sails as a unit. In much the same way, I believe individual schools within a district can "sail under their own power," but the "fleet" of schools must be coordinated and unified to achieve district-wide results.

Second, there is also a serious problem, in my mind, with charter schools: they create pockets of excellence within a district and do not transform entire school districts into high-performing learning organizations. These pockets of excellence are good for the children who are being educated within them. But what about the children in the "noncharter" schools? How is the quality of their education improved? How can an entire district be transformed using the charter school model?

Although SBM and charter schools are innovations in the field of education, from an organization design perspective, they are simply variations of Weber's and Fayol's principles that maintain bureaucracy. A new form of organization design is needed to transform school systems into high-performing knowledge-creating organizations that can succeed in educating children for success in our twenty-first-century society.

The participants in the cluster-based redesign workshops analyze the design of their cluster and create ideas for transforming their organization design into one appropriate for our twenty-first-century Knowledge Age society; that is, they propose ideas to increase their cluster's ability to learn as a system, to provide people with opportunities to succeed, to respond quickly to changes in their external environment, and to provide the children in their care with a high-quality education. These ideas are included in the comprehensive transformation proposal that each CRT submits to the SLT.

Finally, it is important to remember that the internal social infrastructure has a direct and powerful effect on people and how they do their work. A school system can have a state-of-the-art instructional program supported by the best technology, but if their teachers are dissatisfied and demotivated, those educators will not use that instructional program in remarkable ways. The internal social infrastructure must be transformed at the same time that the core and support work processes and environmental relationships are being transformed.

CONCLUSION

It should be clear to readers at this point that KWS Step 2 is a complex set of activities. However, as I mentioned earlier, complex doesn't mean impossible—it only means that there is a lot of thinking and doing that must happen.

It is also important to remember that each cluster—academic and support work—engages in its "personalized" transformation process; that is, each cluster is empowered and enabled to create ideas to transform in ways that are best suited for the cluster. Allowing this personalized approach to transformation to occur is an example of a key system design principle called equifinality. The equifinality principle (Bertalanffy, 1968; Cummings & Worley, 2013) states that in open systems (like a school system) goals can be achieved by many potential and acceptable means. When clusters are empowered to implement the equifinality principle, they tend to create ideas for change that are very relevant to their situation and that tend to stimulate ownership of the changes. However, it is very important to remember that whatever ideas that are created by the clusters must comply with the broad redesign parameters established in the earlier System Engagement Conference. Those parameters were set to accommodate the equifinality principle but also to put a fence around that concept by defining what is permissible and impermissible. The parameters set the stage for creating strategic alignment, which is the focus of the next chapter.

REFERENCES

American Society for Training and Development. (1983). *Models for excellence.* Washington, DC: ASTD, 1–20.

Argyris, C. and Schön, D. (1978). *Organizational learning: A theory of action perspective.* Reading, MA: Addison Wesley.

Balfanz, R., and Herzog, L. (2005, March). *Keeping middle grades students on track to graduation: Initial analysis and implications* in Kennelly, L. and Monrad, M. (2007). Approaches to dropout prevention: Heeding early warning signs with appropriate interventions. Retrieved March 1, 2016 from: http://files.eric.ed.gov/fulltext/ED499009.pdf.

Cogan, M. L. (1973). *Clinical supervision.* Boston: Houghton Mifflin.

Cummings, T. and Worley, C. (2013). *Organization development and change (10th ed.).* Mason, OH: South-Western/Cengage Learning.

Duffy, F. M. (1996). *Designing high performance schools: A practical guide to organizational reengineering.* Del Ray Beach, FL: St. Lucie Press.

Duffy, F. M. (2011). A personal vision for transforming America's education system and 20 laws of transformation to guide the process. *The F.M. Duffy Reports, 16*(3), 1–12. Retrieved on January 13, 2016, from: http://thefmduffygroup.com/publications/reports/FMDuffyReports_Vol16_No3_PersonalVision.pdf.

Duffy, F. M. and Chance, P. L. (2007). *Strategic communication during whole system change: Advice and guidance for school district leaders and PR specialists.* Leading Systemic School Improvement Series, No. 9. Lanham, MD: Rowman & Littlefield Education.

Emery, M. (1993). Participative design: Work and community life. In Emery (Ed.) *Participative design for participative democracy.* Australia: The Australian National University, Centre for Continuing Education.

Emery, F.E. and Thorsrud, E. (1976). *Democracy at work: The report of the Norwegian democracy program.* Leiden, the Netherlands: Nijhoff.

Emery, M. (1993). *Participative design for participative democracy.* Canberra: The Australian National University, Centre for Continuing Education.

Fayol, H. (1949). *General and industrial management.* Constance Storrs, translator. London: Pittman.

Fulmer, R.M., Gibbs, P., and Keys, J.B. (1998). The second generation learning organizations: new tools for sustaining competitive advantage. *Organizational Dynamics, 27*(3), 6–21.

Goldhammer, R. (1969). *Clinical supervision: Special methods for the supervision of teachers.* New York: Holt, Rinehart and Winston.

Hammer, M. and Champy, J. (1993). *Reengineering the corporation: A manifesto for business revolution.* New York: HarperCollins.

Karlin, D. (2007). People tend to support what they help to build. *Fast Company.* Retrieved on January 12, 2016, from: http://www.fastcompany.com/660229/people-tend-support-what-they-help-build.

Likert, R. (1961). *New patterns of management.* New York: McGraw-Hill.

Lipnack, J. and Stamps, J. (1993). *The TeamNet factor*. Essex Junction, VT: Oliver Wight.

McCombs, B. L. (2008). From one-size-fits-all to personalized learner-centered learning: The evidence. *The F. M. Duffy Reports, 13*(2), 1–12.

Nonaka, I. and Takeuchi, H. (1995). *The knowledge-creating company*. New York: Oxford University Press.

Pasmore, W. A. (1992). Sociotechnical systems design for total quality. San Francisco, CA: Organizational Consultants.

Pasmore, W. A. (1988). *Designing effective organizations: The sociotechnical systems perspective*. New York: Wiley & Sons.

Pava, C. H. R. (1983). *Managing new office technology: An organizational strategy*. New York: The New Press.

Preskill, H. and Torres, R. T. (1999). *Evaluative inquiry for learning in organizations*. Thousand Oaks, CA: Sage.

Quinn, J. B., Anderson, P., and Finkelstein, S. (1996 March-April). Managing professional intellect: Making the most of the best. *Harvard Business Review, 74*(2), 71–80.

Reigeluth, C. M. (2013). Instructional theory and technology for the new paradigm of education. *The F. M. Duffy Reports, 18*(4), 1–21. Retrieved on January 13, 2016, from: http://thefmduffygroup.com/publications/reports/FMDuffyReports_Vol18_No4_InstructionalTheoryandTechnology.pdf.

Reigeluth, C.M. and Karnopp, J. R. (2013). *Reinventing schools: It's time to break the mold*. Lanham, MD: Rowman & Littlefield Education.

Robinson, D. G. and Robinson, J. C. (1996). *Performance consulting: Moving beyond training*. San Francisco: Berrett-Koehler, p. 152–153.

Stufflebeam, D. L. (2007). CIPP evaluation model checklist: A tool for applying the fifth Installment of the CIPP Model to assess long-term enterprises. Retrieved on January 14, 2016, from: http://oceanleadership.org/wp-content/uploads/2011/07/cippchecklist-Attch-2.pdf.

Thorndike, E. L. (1905). Law of effect. Retrieved on January 15, 2016, from: http://www.scribd.com/doc/293769831/Law-of-Effect#scribd.

Van Fleet, D. D., Griffin, R. W., and Moorhead, G. (1991). *Behavior in organizations*. Boston: Houghton Mifflin.

Weber, M. (1947). *The theory of social and economic organization*. A.M. Henderson and Talcott Parsons, translators. New York: Oxford University Press.

Weisbord, M. R. and Janoff, S. (1995). *Future Search: An action guide to finding common ground in organizations and communities*. San Francisco, CA: Berrett-Koehler.

Chapter Six

Step 3: Create Strategic Alignment

Knowledge Work Supervision (KWS) is a five-step process that begins with Step 1 focusing on pre-launch preparation activities and then progresses to Step 2 that focuses on the redesign of an entire school system by transforming its relationship with its environment, its core and support work processes, and its internal social infrastructure. Once changes are made, KWS Step 3 seeks to create strategic alignment which helps to stabilize and diffuse the changes throughout the system. KWS Step 4 focuses on the evaluation of the change process and its outcomes. Finally, in Step 5 change-leaders recycle the KWS process to Step 1. This chapter provides guidance for KWS Step 3: Create Strategic Alignment.

CREATING STRATEGIC ALIGNMENT

Strategic alignment is a systematic way to ensure that everyone working in a school system is supporting the system's transformation goals and grand vision. Strategic alignment is created by linking people, priorities, practices, and processes with the districts' strategic goals and grand vision. More than anything else, strategic alignment is a structured and systematic way of ensuring that everyone in a district is committed to achieving the district's new vision by making a contribution and adding value to the education and support provided to children.

The importance of strategic alignment was commented upon by Rummler and Brache (1995). They said,

> We have found that everything in an organization's internal and external 'ecosystem' (customers, products and services, reward systems, technology, organization structure, and so on) is connected. To improve organization and individual performance, we need to understand these connections. (p. 15)

Schwan and Spady (1998, online document) also talked about the importance of strategic alignment in their comments about why strategic change failed in school districts. They said,

> What's missing in most cases is a concrete, detailed vision statement that describes what the organization will look like when operating at its ideal best to accomplish its declared purpose, as well as a systematic process we call strategic alignment. Strategic alignment occurs when the structure, policies, procedures, and practices of the organization totally support the organization's vision.

They continued by observing,

> The alignment of the organizational vision with the actions of those who are part of the organization is a critical step in creating real and lasting change. Such alignment is best fostered and ensured through the supervision process. Every supervisor in the district—from the superintendent to the teacher—is a linking pin. Every individual links one part of the organization to another. If the vision is lost by any pin, implementation of the vision becomes an option for anyone supervised by that pin, and in turn for anyone who reports to that pin's supervisees.

The KWS methodology supports Schwan and Spady's beliefs about the role of supervision as a process to create strategic alignment but KWS, as noted throughout the book, shifts the focus of supervision off individual teachers and on to the entire system.

GETTING ALL THE HORSES TO PULL THE WAGON IN THE SAME DIRECTION

Creating strategic alignment is like getting a team of horses to pull a wagon in the same direction. You can't have each horse trying to pull the wagon in a different direction. In much the same way, change-leaders in school districts cannot have teams, schools, academic and support work clusters, and individuals all doing their "own thing" with total disregard for their district's strategic goals and grand vision. This is not exactly an effective way to transform a school system.

The Meaning of Strategic Alignment

Once a school district is transformed, change-leaders devise strategies to align the work of individuals with the goals of their teams, the work of teams with the goals of their schools, the work of schools with the goals of their clusters, and the work of clusters with the goals of the district. These linkages are the essence of strategic alignment (Duffy, 2004).

Strategic alignment also requires vertical and horizontal linkages. Vertical alignment creates vertical linkages like those noted in the preceding paragraph. Horizontal alignment connects clusters with other clusters, schools and support work units with other schools and support work units, and individuals with other individuals.

A process tool known as "outside-in analysis" (Beckhard, 1983) is used throughout the strategic alignment process. This tool is used to examine district-level policies and procedures to ensure that these things will help people succeed in transforming their clusters, schools and support work units, and teams. Further, any policy, regulation, or standard operating procedure that is identified as an obstacle for the transformation process (e.g., obstructionist policies, faulty procedures, and so on) must be removed or modified starting at the level of the school board and moving inward toward the performance of individual teachers. Sometimes these obstacles will be put in place by state or federal legislation. In these situations change-leaders may be able to petition their state departments of education for waivers from the obstructionist requirements.

The reason for this "outside-in" alignment sequence is that by doing it this way, change-leaders create an internal social infrastructure within which the performance of teams and individuals is supported by conditions for success (e.g., the removal of "red tape") and resources they need to succeed. Then, if teams and individuals are not performing as expected, they have no excuse for less-than-expected performance levels and they can be held accountable for not performing as expected.

Creating strategic alignment, as described above, accomplishes three things: First, it ensures that everyone is working toward the same district-level broad strategic goals and grand vision. Second, it weaves a web of accountabilities that makes everyone who directly or indirectly touches the educational experience of a child accountable for his or her part in shaping that experience. And third, it removes (by using the outside-in process) bureaucratic hassles, dysfunctional policies, and obstructionist procedures that limit individual and team effectiveness. Deming (1982), among others, said that it is these hassles, policies, and procedures that cause at least 80 percent of the performance problems that are usually blamed on individuals and teams.

Components of an Effective Strategic Alignment Process

An effective strategic alignment process has several components, each of which is essential for achieving alignment (Duffy, 2004). These are summarized below:

District-Wide Planning

Vision and mission. During KWS Step 2, a new core purpose, a mission, values, and goals are defined for the school system. The purpose, mission, and values act as beacons shining light on the path toward a district's future. The goals serve as trail markers to ensure that everyone in the district is headed in the same direction. These system variables also provide the broad context for evaluating system performance.

Strategic plan. Change-leaders also develop a new strategic plan for their district during KWS Step 2. A strategic plan defines and communicates how a district's mission and vision will be achieved through transformation and provides direction to clusters, schools, support work units, and individuals.

Although a strategic plan is needed to set a course, it is important to remember that systemic change is not a sequential, linear process. In fact, it's quite nonlinear and chaotic. So, it is crucial that change-leaders do not assume that their strategic plan by itself will take them to their desired future.

Operating plans. Each cluster, school, and support work unit in a district needs to create a plan of operation that connects its work to the district's strategic goals and vision. These operational plans need to be communicated broadly to all employees so they can then align their individual performance with their teams' goals.

Individual and Team Planning

Individual and team planning is where people align their performance with higher-level goals.

Individual performance plans. Each individual, working collaboratively with his or her team leader, principal, or supervisor, develops measurable performance objectives that are aligned with his or her team, school, or support work unit goals. These objectives define what results are to be achieved, how these results are to be achieved, what resources are needed to perform effectively and how the resources will be used, and how performance will serve internal and external customers.

Team performance plans. All teams develop measurable performance objectives. These plans must be aligned with school, cluster, and district goals. Information from individual performance plans is also found in the team plans but modified to reflect team goals and performance expectations.

Communication and Feedback

Multi-directional communication systems. One of the key improvements made to a district during KWS Step 2 is the redesign of its internal social infrastructure. Social infrastructure includes organization design, organization culture, the reward system, communication policies and procedures, informal norms, and so on. Each of these variables must be assessed and transformed if necessary.

Another change made to the internal social infrastructure using KWS is the creation of a network of teams. To make this network effective, it is important to establish norms and procedures for multidirectional communication. A transformed school district should have a communication plan for disseminating information throughout the system about the district's strategic direction, philosophy, values, policies, procedures, and performance and for involving faculty and staff in the transformation journey. An effective communication plan should also use multimedia communication tools: written memoranda, audio–visual presentations and live, stand-up presentations, Facebook, Twitter, and so on.

Performance feedback systems. Everyone, including administrators and supervisors, must receive regular performance feedback. Informal one-on-one sessions and team reviews provide opportunities for frequent conversations about individual and team performance. Traditional instructional supervision can play a role here, especially clinical supervision as it was originally conceived.

Principles, Tools, and Methods for Orchestrating Strategic Alignment

When change-leaders are trying to create strategic alignment within their district, they ask and answer a few simple questions:

- What are the strategic goals of the district? What is its vision?
- Do the performance goals and activities of the academic and support work clusters, schools, support work units, communities of practice, and individuals clearly support the district's vision and strategic goals?
- If "yes," how do we reward and reinforce that alignment?
- If "no," why not? And, what do we do about it?
- Who's accountable for alignment or misalignment? What are the consequences (positive or negative) for either creating alignment or for not creating it?

Using Implementation Feedback as Formative Evaluation

Implementation feedback is where change-leaders take a good look at how the improvements they are making in clusters, schools, and teams are being implemented. They also give people feedback on their performance and on whether or not new policies, procedures, and relationships are working as intended. Then, they expect people to take the necessary actions either to reinforce what they're doing right or to correct what they're doing wrong. People are then held accountable for taking these actions.

Cummings and Worley (2013) discussed the importance of implementation feedback for organization development purposes. They said,

> Most OD [organization development] interventions require significant changes in people's behaviors and ways of thinking about organizations. Implementing such changes requires considerable learning and experimentation as employees and managers discover how to translate these general prescriptions [the required changes] into specific behaviors and procedures. This learning process involves much trial and error and needs to be guided by information about whether behaviors and procedures are being changed as intended. (p. 175)

Since KWS is an organization development intervention and since creating strategic alignment is an important goal for this intervention, implementation feedback becomes a primary tool for creating strategic alignment. This happens within the context of "On-Track Seminars" designed using the principles of evaluative inquiry (Preskill & Torres, 1999).

Another important reason for using implementation feedback is related to one of the core principles of sociotechnical systems design: minimal specificity (Cummings & Worley, 2001). This principle advises change-leaders to define minimally the specifics of desired improvements. In applying this principle, then, individuals and teams have the freedom and authority to add specificity as needed. This freedom to add specificity, however, creates a problem for a school district because as specificity is added, intentional and unintentional deviations from what was expected occur. Thus, to achieve strategic alignment, change-leaders have to bring everything back into alignment. Implementation feedback helps do this.

Weave and Strum a Web of Accountabilities

It's ineffective to hold classroom teachers and support personnel solely responsible for work outcomes. Instead, change-leaders need to adopt the mental model of a web of accountabilities (Merrifield, 1998). They weave this web by using a network of self-managing teams that are all focused on helping their district achieve its new mission and grand vision which were conceived in KWS Step 2 in a System Engagement Conference. The performance of individual teachers, administrators, and support staff must also be woven into this web. Once woven, the web is strummed so all in it feel the vibration of accountability pulsing through their individual and collective conscious. Everyone in the web must clearly realize the consequences of nonperformance, and they must also clearly realize the rewards associated with success and high performance (which is one of the reasons why a school system's reward system must be retooled during KWS Step 2).

Sustaining Strategic Alignment

By completing KWS, educators transform their school systems and then align the work of individuals, teams, schools, support work units, and clusters with the strategic direction and grand vision of their district. After strategic alignment is achieved, the overall performance of the district is evaluated to determine if the system is performing as intended. This is done during KWS Step 4: Evaluate System Performance. Chapter 9 provides guidance on evaluating whole-system change using principles of summative evaluation (Stufflebeam, 2000).

After educators work their way through KWS, they then focus on institutionalizing the changes that were made by managing the performance of the district, clusters, schools, support work units, teams, and individuals using principles of continuous improvement. After a predetermined period, educators then move to Step 5 by recycling the KWS process to Step 1: Pre-Launch Preparation.

Benefits of Creating and Maintaining Strategic Alignment

By creating and maintaining strategic alignment, a school district may experience the following benefits:

1. greater success as people, priorities, practices, and processes are aligned with a district's strategic goals and vision;
2. improved service to students and their parents because of aligned and synchronized work processes, a more satisfying and motivating work environment for employees, and stronger relationships with external stakeholders;
3. increased effectiveness for individuals and teams because they will be spending less time correcting problems they didn't cause, they will be engaged in effective communication, and they will become an integral strand in a powerful web of accountabilities; and
4. greater job satisfaction and motivation because of a redesigned social infrastructure that increases the level of authentic participation, ownership of improvement plans and goals, shared responsibility for student outcomes, and higher and sustainable levels of intrinsic motivation.

CONCLUSION

Creating strategic alignment ensures that everyone in a school district is moving in the same general direction during times of transformation. School districts must have a mission, vision, and strategic direction and every person, program, policy, and procedure must be aligned with that vision and direction. Although each school, classroom, and support work unit is where important improvements happen, faculty and staff in those units cannot each be "doing their own thing." Surely, teachers in a school may use a special teaching technique that no one else in the district uses. Certainly, a building principal should have the authority to manage his or her school and its resources. But no school, no teacher, no staff person, and no administrator should be permitted to perform in ways that diverge significantly from his or her district's mission, vision, and strategic direction. All the horses must pull the wagon in the same direction.

REFERENCES

Beckhard, R. (1983). Strategies for large system change. In W. L. French, C. H. Bell, Jr., and R. A. Zawacki (Eds.). *Organization development: Theory, practice, and research.* Plano, TX: Business : 234–242.

Cummings, T. and Worley, C. (2013). *Organization development and change (10th ed.).* Mason, OH: South-Western/Cengage Learning.

Deming, W. E. (1982). *Out of crisis.* Cambridge, MA: MIT Press.

Duffy, F. M. (2002). *Step-up-to-excellence: An innovative approach to managing and rewarding performance in school systems.* Lanham, MD: Scarecrow Education

Duffy, F. M. (2003) *Courage, passion, and vision: A guide to leading systemic school improvement.* Lanham, MD: Scarecrow Education and the American Association of School Administrators.

Duffy, F. M. (2004). *Moving upward together: Creating strategic alignment to sustain change.* Leading Systemic School Improvement Series, No.1. Lanham, MD: Scarecrow Education.

Duffy, F. M. and Dale, J. D. (Eds.). (2001). *Creating successful school systems: Voices from the university, the field, and the community.* Norwood, MA: Christopher Gordon.

Emery, M. (1993) (Ed.). *Participative design for participative democracy.* Canberra, Australia: Australian National University.

Merrifield, J. (1998, July). *Contested ground: Performance accountability in adult basic education.* Cambridge, MA: The National Center for the Study of Adult Learning and Literacy.

Preskill, H. and Torres, R. T. (1999). *Evaluative inquiry for learning in organizations.* Thousand Oaks, CA: Sage.

Rummler G.A. and Brache, A. P. (1995). *Improving performance: How to manage the white space on the organization chart (2nd ed.)*. San Francisco: Jossey-Bass.

Schwan, C. and Spady, W. (1998). Why change doesn't happen and how to make sure it does. *Educational Leadership* 55(7). ERIC Number: EJ563902.

Stufflebeam, D. L. (2000). The CIPP model for evaluation. In D. L. Stufflebeam, G. F. Madaus, and T, Kellaghan (Eds.). *Evaluation models: Viewpoints on educational and human services evaluation*. Boston: Kluwer Academic, pp. 279–317.

Chapter Seven

Step 4: Evaluate Whole-System Transformation

Educators have traditionally responded to external pressure for change by using linear school improvement models that expect change-leaders to (1) create a vision of the future, (2) assess the current situation, (3) compare the present to the desired future and identify the gaps, (4) set goals and objectives to move from the present to the future, and (5) move straight forward toward that future. This traditional approach to change was developed by Lewin (1951).

Reality, however, has an annoying way of interfering with good plans. Unexpected events and unintended consequences create three unpredictable change-paths (transform environmental relationships, transform core and support work processes, and transform internal social infrastructure) that are river-like rather than linear. Good intentions and inspiring visions flee the confusion of an unpredictable reality causing people to revert quickly to their "old ways of doing things." The consequence of this experience is captured in the eloquent French folk wisdom: "The more things change, the more they stay the same."

Given these challenges, and the complexity of navigating large-scale change, it is imperative that change-leaders evaluate the process and outcomes of their transformation effort. What follows are some ideas about how to do that.

EFFECTIVENESS MEANS OF ACHIEVING GOALS

Transformation goals are statements about what change-leaders want their school system to become—a future state of being. Effectiveness, in the context of transformational change, is the degree to which a school system achieves its transformation goals. Effectiveness is also a broad concept that takes into consideration not only the whole system, but also its component units. Thus, effectiveness measures the degree to which all parts of a transforming school system are achieving their respective goals. There are two basic approaches to measuring effectiveness: contingency approaches and balanced effectiveness approaches (Daft, 2001, p. 64). Let's take a brief look at each approach.

Contingency Approaches to Measuring Effectiveness

Contingency approaches to measuring effectiveness assume that school systems function as open systems. As open systems, school systems need resources from their environments to support their transformation journey. These resources enter a school system and are used to move the system toward a desirable future—a future conceived in the early phases of Knowledge Work Supervision (KWS) Step 2: Redesign the Entire System. These contingency approaches to evaluating effectiveness use one of three methods that judge a school system's transformation effectiveness:

- the goal approach (evaluates the outcomes of transformation);
- the resource-based approach (evaluates the level of resources provided by the environment to support the transformation); and
- the internal process approach (evaluates the transformation process itself).

Goal Approach

The goal approach evaluates a school system's transformation goals and then assesses how well the system and its component parts (clusters of interconnected schools and support work units) achieved those goals. The important goals to examine using this approach are called operative goals, rather than official goals.

Operative goals describe specific measurable outcomes and are often focused on short-term achievements (Daft, 2001, p. 53). Official goals, on the other hand, are the formally stated description of what a school system hopes to achieve by transforming. These are often referred to as a school system's mission and vision statements. Official goals tend to be more abstract and difficult to measure. Efforts to measure goal achievement are more productive when operative goals are used rather than official goals (Hall & Clark, 1980).

The goal approach is very useful for school systems with transformation goals that can be easily measured; for example, "Did the system meet its deadlines?" "Did the change-leaders organize a Community Engagement

Conference?" However, identifying operative goals and measuring school system performance against those goals is not always easy because of two thorny problems: multiple goals and subjective indicators of goal achievement.

Multiple goals. When a school system has multiple transformation goals, effectiveness cannot be determined on the basis of a single indicator. High achievement on one goal may result in lower achievement on another. Furthermore, each academic and support work unit in a school system also has transformation goals. So, the full assessment of a school system's effectiveness in achieving transformation goals must take these multiple goals into consideration. To manage the evaluation of multiple goals, organizations in other sectors of our society use a balanced approach to measurement (described later) that use multiple points of evaluation; for example, some businesses set goals for financial performance, customer service and satisfaction, internal processes, and innovation and learning (Fritsch, 1997).

Subjective indicators of goal achievement. Someone has to decide which goals are important to measure and which are not. When these kinds of decisions are made, subjectivity comes into play. In fact, when it comes to evaluation, I believe there is no such thing as objectivity. All evaluators apply some degree of personal subjectivity for making evaluative decisions. Evaluation is, after all, a process of attaching value and worth to something or someone. Since there is no such thing as objectivity here, the challenge for evaluators is managing their subjectivity.

The goals approach is important, but it has weaknesses. It doesn't evaluate the transformation process and ignores the relationship the school system needs to have with its external environment.

Internal Process Approach

This approach examines internal efficiency (not effectiveness). Efficiency is a measure of how many precious resources are used to achieve transformation goals. If an inordinate amount of resources are used to achieve a few goals, then the transforming system is evaluated as inefficient. If resources are used wisely and with little waste, then the transforming system is evaluated as efficient.

An efficient transformation process is one that creates critically important changes to a school system's environmental relationships, core and support work processes, and internal social infrastructure by using valuable resources wisely. However, the internal process approach to evaluation also has shortcomings. It doesn't consider how effectively a school system achieves its goals and doesn't evaluate a system's relationship with its environment.

Resource-Based Approach

This approach assumes that school systems must be successful in obtaining the human, technical, and financial resources needed to support their transformation journey. From this perspective, organizational effectiveness is defined as "the ability of the organization ... to obtain scarce and valued resources and successfully integrate and manage them" (Russo & Fouts, 1997).

This approach is useful when other indicators of effectiveness are difficult to determine. During times of transformation it may be challenging to measure output goals (goal approach) and internal efficiency (internal process approach). Thus, looking at how successful a school system is in acquiring valuable and scarce resources could be a good indicator of their transformation effectiveness. For example, if a school system is succeeding in getting all the money it needs for its transformation budget, then this level of "available resources" might indicate how much faith external stakeholders have in the school system's ability to transform.

This approach has shortcomings too, one of which is that it barely considers the needs of a school system's stakeholders—the ones not providing financial resources. The ability to secure resources is good, but it is only good if a school system is using the resources to respond to the needs, issues, and concerns of key stakeholders.

BALANCED APPROACHES TO MEASURING EFFECTIVENESS

KWS is used to transform entire school systems by making simultaneous improvements in three key areas: the system's relationship with the outside world, its core and support work processes, and its internal social infrastructure. The *goal attainment approach* to evaluating effectiveness is coupled to work processes, the *internal process method* is linked to internal social infrastructure, and the *resource approach* is connected to improving environmental relationships. But, with KWS, the school system's effectiveness in all three areas needs to be evaluated. Evaluating system performance in all three areas can be challenging, but it is possible using a "balanced approach" to measuring effectiveness.

Each of the contingency approaches for measuring effectiveness described above has something to offer, but each one gives only partial answers to evaluation questions. So, a balanced approach is used to evaluate a school system's overall success in its transformation journey. The balanced approach also acknowledges that the system does many things and has multiple outcomes. These balanced approaches combine several indicators of effectiveness into a single evaluation framework. The two main methods that are part of the balanced approach to measuring effectiveness are the *stakeholder approach* and the *competing values approach*.

The Stakeholder Approach

An entire school system is transformed using KWS. During KWS Step 1, the pre-launch team engages their system's stakeholders in a large group process called a *Community Engagement Conference*, which is designed using the principles of Open Space Technology. The purpose of this activity is to determine the expectations that various stakeholders have for the school system and to solicit their ideas for transforming the school system.

Later in KWS Step 2, change-leaders engage internal stakeholders (teachers, administrators, support staff) in another large group process called a *System Engagement Conference*, which is based on the principles of the Weisbord and Janoff's (1995) "Future Search" conference. The purpose of this conference is to develop a new mission, a new vision, and new strategic goals for a system. The stakeholder approach can be used during either of these large group sessions to assess the satisfaction of both external and internal stakeholders. Their level of satisfaction can be interpreted as an indicator of effectiveness (Tsui, 1990).

The usefulness of the stakeholder approach is that it views effectiveness broadly and assesses factors in a school system's environment as well as within the system. This approach is popular because it views effectiveness as a complex, multidimensional concept that has no single measure (Cameron, 1984). Considering the social and political environment that school systems find themselves within, along with high-stakes pressure to increase student achievement as indicated on state-mandated assessments, this approach seems to be one that could be useful.

Competing Values Approach

This approach is comprised of four models for judging effectiveness: the human relations model, the open systems model, the internal process model, and the rational goal model. I will talk briefly about each one in a moment, but first I provide some background information about these models.

Research on goals and criteria set by practitioners indicates that their views of organizational effectiveness often conflict with researchers' views (Quinn & Rohrbaugh, 1983). Quinn and Rohrbaugh developed the competing values approach to measuring effectiveness by combining the views of practitioners and researchers. They used a panel of experts in organizational effectiveness to identify and classify effectiveness indicators developed by practitioners and another list of indicators developed by researchers. Indicators on both lists were rated for similarity. The final analysis yielded a list of effectiveness indicators representing competing values in organizations (practitioners' versus researchers').

Quinn and Rohrbaugh's study indicated that managers have values for relating to their organization's external environment or values for relating to the people who work in their organization. This external–internal dimension is called "focus." A second dimension the researchers identified is "structure." Managers either value stability or flexibility. Stability refers to a management value for efficiency and top–down control. Flexibility, on the other hand, represents a management value for learning and change.

If the structure dimension (stability–flexibility) is imagined as a vertical line that intersects with a horizontal line representing the focus dimension (internal–external), a grid with four quadrants is formed. Inside each quadrant is an effectiveness model that complements the dominant management values for that quadrant. Here's a brief description of the effectiveness model in each quadrant. These models are the ones that comprise the competing values approach.

Human Relations Model of Effectiveness (Internal Focus with Value for Flexibility)

With this model, managers focus on developing their system's human resources. Employees are given opportunities for autonomy and development. Managers work toward goals of cohesion, morale, and training opportunities. Systems adopting this model are more concerned with their employees than with the environment.

Internal Process Model of Effectiveness (Internal Focus with Value for Stability)

With this model, managers seek a stable organizational setting that maintains itself in an orderly fashion. Organizations that are comfortably situated in their environments with no pressure to change adopt a model like this. Managers using this model work toward goals for efficient communication, information management, and decision-making.

Open Systems Model of Effectiveness (External Focus with Value for Flexibility)

Using this model, managers' primary goals are for growth and resource acquisition. These primary goals are achieved through subgoals for flexibility, readiness, and a positive evaluation by external stakeholders. The dominant value in this model is for establishing a good relationship with the organization's environment.

Rational Goal Model (External Focus with Value for Stability and Control)

The primary effectiveness goals in this model are for productivity, efficiency, and profit. The focus is on achieving output goals in a controlled, rational manner. Subgoals focus on internal planning and goal setting, which are rational management tools.

The above models represent different perspectives on how to evaluate the overall effectiveness of a school system and its clusters, schools, and teams. Change-leaders will need to decide which model best complements their system and its change management philosophy.

EVALUATIVE INQUIRY FOR LEARNING IN ORGANIZATIONS

On-Track Seminars, designed using principles of a formative evaluation method called implementation feedback, are used to create strategic alignment (see chapter 6). The purpose of formative evaluation is to provide periodic performance feedback to people so they can align their work with the transformation goals of their respective units and with the broad strategic goals and vision of their system. These formative evaluations are done during KWS Steps 2–4. A formative evaluation method that I really like was developed by Preskill and Torres (1999) called "evaluative inquiry for learning in organizations." Their methodology is also highly compatible with KWS, and it is used to design On-Track Seminars that are used throughout the KWS process to provide change-leaders with formative evaluation data to keep the transformation on track.

Preskill and Torres' evaluative inquiry model is perfectly suited to the KWS protocol. I used their model to create the On-Track Seminar, which is a formative evaluation tool used with KWS. In describing the context for evaluative inquiry they said,

> Continuous organizational change is resulting in less organizational stability and a redefinition of who we are and what we do in the workplace. The traditional structures that have given us a feeling of solidity and predictability have vanished. This shift has placed a greater emphasis on the need for fluid processes that can change as an organization and its members' needs change. Instead of the

traditional rational, linear, hierarchical approach to managing jobs, which focused on breaking down job tasks and isolating job functions, tomorrow's jobs will be built on establishing networks of relationships. (Preskill & Torres, 1999, p. xvii)

According to Preskill and Torres, their evaluative inquiry model not only helps gather information for decision making and action, but it also helps to question and debate the value of what a system is doing. Preskill and Torres' model offers a tool for questioning completely everything that a system does—everything! There are no sacred cows. They said,

> We envision evaluative inquiry as an on-going process for investigating and understanding critical organizational issues. It is an approach to learning that is fully integrated with an organization's work practices [i.e., a system's knowledge work processes], and as such, it engenders (a) organization members' interest and ability in exploring critical issues using evaluation logic, (b) organization members' involvement in evaluative processes, and (c) the personal and professional growth of individuals in the organization. (Preskill & Torres, 1999, p. 2)

In the above quote, a, b, and c are all components of a system's internal social infrastructure, which is transformed during KWS Step 2.

Evaluative inquiry has three phases and incorporates four key learning processes. The phases are: Phase 1—Focusing the Evaluative Inquiry, Phase 2—Carrying Out the Inquiry, and Phase 3—Applying Learning. During each of the phases, organization members and stakeholders come together to engage in a learning process that incorporates four key learning processes: dialogue; reflection; asking questions; and identifying and clarifying values, beliefs, assumptions, and knowledge. The KWS methodology accommodates these phases and processes.

Preskill and Torres also outlined the organizational structures needed to facilitate the use of evaluative inquiry. All of the following can be created when redesigning a system's internal social infrastructure using KWS:

- support for collaboration, communication, and cooperation among organization members as well as across units or departments;
- help for organization members to understand how their roles relate to other roles in the organization and to the organization's mission as a whole (i.e., they create alignment);
- recognition of individuals and their capacity to learn as an organization's greatest resource; and
- value for the whole person and support for personal as well as professional development using reward systems that recognize team as well as individual learning and performance (p. 172).

FROM FORMATIVE TO SUMMATIVE EVALUATION

In KWS Step 5, change-leaders begin applying principles of summative evaluation. There is a lot of literature on program evaluation, so I am not going to go into great detail about this approach. Also, please know that I am not an evaluation expert. However, people like Scriven (2001) and Stufflebeam (2000) are experts and a lot of helpful guidance about evaluation can be found from people like them. But, in the meantime, let's take a quick look at summative evaluation and how it can be used to evaluate the overall effectiveness of a school system and its clusters, schools, and teams.

Summative evaluation provides data and information about how a school system is performing over time. These evaluation measures must also be aligned with stakeholder expectations, which often come in the form of performance standards. By aligning evaluations with stakeholder expectations, change-leaders position their system to be viewed in a positive light by those stakeholders because they are giving them the data and information they want.

Context, Inputs, Processes and Products Evaluation

The summative evaluation model called Context, Inputs, Processes, and Product (CIPP) Evaluation (Stufflebeam, 2000) is based on principles of systems theory and complements the KWS methodology, which is also based on systems theory. The CIPP model also combines principles of formative and summative evaluation, so change-leaders can use parts of it during Steps 2–4 of the KWS methodology to create strategic alignment.

All organizations exist within a context (C). Units within an organization exist within a context too. All organizations and their units need resources which are called inputs (I) in the language of systems theory. All organizations use processes (P) to convert the inputs into something meaningful and useful for customers. The "something" created are products (P). So, when change-leaders want to evaluate organizational and unit effectiveness they evaluate their system's context, inputs, processes, and products (i.e., CIPP). This is a core principle of the CIPP model, and it is a systems view of organizational and unit performance.

Stufflebeam's (2000) CIPP evaluation model offers a systematic way to collect, analyze, and report data about the effectiveness of a school system and its clusters, schools, and teams. The CIPP model is not a new approach to evaluation. But it is one that is based on a systems perspective of organizations and, as such, is very appropriate to use with KWS.

While space constraints do not permit a full explanation of how to use the CIPP model, I will briefly discuss how it can provide useful performance data about a system's effectiveness. As noted above, the CIPP methodology is composed of four related evaluations: an evaluation of (1) context, (2) inputs, (3) processes, and (4) products. Data from these four evaluations provide answers to several basic questions:

What Should We Do?

Answers to this question will guide efforts to transform a school system and its clusters, schools, and teams. Change-leaders conduct this evaluation by collecting and analyzing needs and opportunities data to determine goals, priorities, and objectives. Two powerful tools that are used in the KWS protocol are exquisitely suited to answering this question. These tools are the *Community Engagement Conference* and the *System Engagement Conference*. Both of these tools will also help identify the expectations held by external stakeholders—the individuals and groups that comprise the context (C) for a school system.

How Should We Do It?

When change-leaders get answers to this question, what they end up with are operative goals and objectives. In the KWS methodology, the primary tool used to answer this question is the *redesign workshop* that engages a school system's faculty and staff in a series of workshops aimed at creating innovative improvements in their system's (1) relationship with its environments, (2) its core and support work processes, and (3) its internal social infrastructure. Seeking answers to this question focuses on identifying the inputs (I) to the system's transformation journey.

Are We Doing It As Planned?

The answers to this question will tell change-leaders (1) if they are implementing all of the wonderful ideas to transform their system that were created in the redesign workshops and (2) if everything is strategically aligned with the system's grand vision and strategic goals. Here, change-leaders assess their system's processes (P) used to transform their systems. Answers to this question are found during KWS Steps 2–4.

Did the Changes Work?

By measuring the actual outcomes and comparing them to desired outcomes, change-leaders are able to decide if the transformation was effective. They do this during Step 5 of the KWS methodology. This is the essence of summative evaluation. When change-leaders answer this question, they are evaluating the products (P) or outcomes of their transformation journey.

CONCLUSION

I like the CIPP model of evaluation because it clearly and powerfully complements the KWS methodology. I also like Preskill and Torres' model for evaluative inquiry as a formative evaluation tool. I believe that both can be conjoined to provide change-leaders with a powerful evaluation methodology for evaluating the context, inputs, processes, and products of KWS by providing formative and summative evaluation data and also producing individual, team, and system learning. Now, that's commanding!

REFERENCES

Cameron, K. S. (1984). The effectiveness of ineffectiveness. In B. M. Staw and L. L. Cummings (Eds.), *Research in organizational behavior*. Greenwich, CT: JAI Press.

Daft, R. L. (2001). *Organization theory and design* (7th ed.). Cincinnati, OH: South-Western College.

Fritsch, M. J. (1997, September–October). Balanced scorecard helps Northern States Power's quality academy achieve extraordinary performance. *Corporate University Review, 22*.

Hall, R. H. and Clark, J. P. (1980). An ineffective effectiveness study and some suggestions for future research. *Sociological Quarterly, 21*, 119–134.

Preskill, H. and Torres, R. T. (1999). *Evaluative inquiry for learning in organizations*. Thousand Oaks, CA: Sage.

Quinn, R. E. and Rohrbaugh, J. (1983). A spatial model of effectiveness criteria: Toward a competing values approach to organizational analysis. *Management Science, 29*, 363–377.

Russo, M. V. and Fouts, P. A. (1997, June). A resource-based perspective on corporate environmental performance and profitability. *Academy of Management Journal, 40*(3), 534–559.

Scriven, M. (2001). Hard-won lessons in program evaluation. Retrieved on March 3, 2016. ERIC Number: EJ478673.

Stufflebeam, D. L. (2000). The CIPP model for evaluation. In D. L. Stufflebeam, G. F. Madaus, and T. Kellaghan (Eds.). *Evaluation models: Viewpoints on educational and human services evaluation*. Boston: Kluwer Academic, pp. 279–317.

Tsui, A. S. (1990). A multiple-constituency model of effectiveness: An empirical examination at the human resource subunit level. *Administrative Science Quarterly, 35*, 458–483.

Weisbord, M. R. and Janoff, S. (1995). *Future Search: An action guide to finding common ground in organizations and communities*. San Francisco, CA: Berrett-Koehler.

Chapter Eight

Step 5: Recycle to Pre-Launch Preparation

Knowledge Work Supervision (KWS) Steps 1–4 are used to transform an entire school system for the purpose of enhancing teachers' professional intellect and for designing school districts to be highly effective knowledge-creating systems. Pasmore (1988, 1992) suggested that large-scale organizational change can range from eighteen to thirty-six months for small- to medium-sized organizations and five to seven years for larger organizations.

After investing so much time and resources to transform a school system, change-leaders must then take steps to stabilize their system, institutionalize the changes, and practice continuous improvement to make adjustments to what was created through KWS. These activities are all part of KWS Step 5. At some point, which will vary from district to district, change-leaders will recognize that it is time to return their system to KWS Step 1 to begin another cycle of transformational change. KWS creates an upward spiral that moves a school system to higher and higher levels of system performance.

In this chapter, I focus on what happens during KWS Step 5 as change-leaders practice continuous improvement (CI). Before discussing CI, I need to point out how CI fits into the KWS protocol. CI follows transformational change—it does not precede or replace transformational change. CI is not a transformation strategy—it is a strategy for making incremental improvements to the quality of a system's performance. Unfortunately, as currently practiced, it is a powerful tool for sustaining the status quo. If change-leaders truly want to transform their systems they first use KWS and then use CI during KWS Step 5.

CONTINUOUS IMPROVEMENT

The purpose of CI, also known as continuous quality improvement (CQI), is to make ongoing, incremental improvements to a system's performance. The origins of the CI process can be traced back to the work of three individuals and the organizations for which they worked. According to Chassin and O'Kane (online, date unknown),

> Beginning in the mid-1920s, Walter A. Shewhart and W. Edwards Deming, both physicists, and Joseph M. Juran, an engineer, laid the groundwork for modern quality improvement. In their efforts to increase the efficiency of American industry, they concentrated on streamlining production processes, while minimizing the opportunity for human error, forging important quality improvement concepts like standardizing work processes, data-driven decision making, and commitment from workers and managers to improving work practice.

Most publications describing the CI process identify a four-phase process: Plan, do, study, and act. Each of the four phases is briefly described below:

Plan. Plans are made to achieve desirable system objectives by making incremental improvements. As a part of KWS Step 5, the CI plan focuses on ensuring that all of the changes that were made during the transformation are working as planned and producing desirable outcomes.

Do. This is the step where the CI plans are implemented and performance data are collected.

Study. As the CI plans are implemented change-leaders pay attention to how the incremental improvements are unfolding, especially focusing on the impact of the CI process and its outcomes.

Act. As the impact of the incremental changes is assessed change-leaders then decide if further action is needed. If the incremental changes produced favorable outcomes, change-leaders continue to implement the CI plan. If the incremental changes were not successful then change-leaders engage in an "after-action" review to determine what they learned. Given what they learned they then start the CI "plan, do, study, and act" process again as part of their continuous improvement efforts.

There is an abundant literature on CI strategies, tools, and processes. Finding advice and guidance on how to practice CI will not be challenging (see Minnesota Office of Continuous Improvement, online, date unknown). However, please remember that CI does not precede or replace transformational change. If change-leaders want to transform their systems, continuous improvement won't work.

DIAGNOSTIC SUPERVISION FOR CONTINUOUS IMPROVEMENT OF TEACHING AND LEARNING

Diagnostic Supervision

Diagnostic supervision is a branch of instructional supervision derived from diagnostic teaching and Cogan's clinical supervision (1972). The "paradigm of diagnostic supervision" was first conceptualized by Lapcevic (1973) and later elaborated by Seager (1974). Figure 8.1 illustrates the paradigm. Seager was a graduate student of Morris Cogan's, the creator of Clinical Supervision, in the Harvard Graduate School of Education. His academic advisor was Robert Anderson. One of Seager's classmates was Robert Goldhammer, who published the first book about Clinical Supervision. Seager was also my academic and dissertation advisor at the University of Pittsburgh between 1975 and 1979. Morris Cogan was one of my professors.

Diagnostic supervision is perfectly aligned with the goal of enhancing teachers' professional intellect through the KWS methodology. Seager (1971) noted, "At its finest, supervision can be a resource to be managed by teachers for the improvement of instruction and for their professional development. Powerful concepts, principles, techniques, and instruments are now available to supervisors and teachers who accept this challenge" (p. 1). By using diagnostic supervision, teachers and traditional instructional supervisors engage in a diagnostic process of supervision that responds to the individual needs,

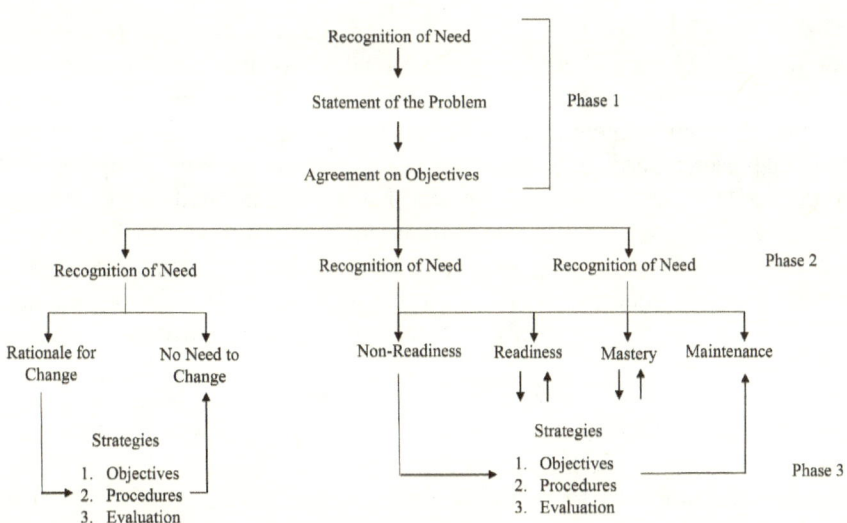

Figure 8.1 Paradigm of Diagnostic Supervision

interests, and abilities of teachers within the context of their school system and community's goals and priorities for educating children. Diagnostic supervision begins by recognizing the teachers' professional needs, stating work-related problems to be addressed, and agreeing on objectives for improving teaching and learning and for the professional growth of the teachers.

While KWS shifts the focus of instructional supervision off individual teachers and on to the overall design and functioning of a school system, diagnostic supervision focuses on helping individual teachers to improve instruction in their classrooms and to enhance their professional intellect. The KWS process becomes extraordinarily powerful as it focuses on transforming an entire school system and then, through diagnostic supervision, refocuses on helping individual teachers to adopt, adapt, and sustain their school system's transformed (1) environmental relationships, (2) core and support work processes, and (3) internal social infrastructure.

Diagnostic supervision has three phases:

- Phase 1—Recognizing needs, stating problems, and agreeing on objectives.
- Phase 2—Assessing attitudes, concepts, and skills.
- Phase 3—Selecting or designing strategies for change.

Phase 1—Recognizing Needs, Stating Problems, and Agreeing on Objectives

The challenging aspect of diagnostic supervision is that the process of improving teaching and growing professionally is conceived of as a process to be managed by a teacher—not by a supervisor. If a teacher is expected to manage the improvement of his or her teaching and professional development then that teacher needs to be empowered and enabled to do that. Empowering a teacher to be self-supervising means that the transformed school system must acknowledge a teacher's opportunity to be self-supervising. Enabling a teacher to be self-supervising means that he or she needs to develop the appropriate attitudes, concepts, and skills to be self-supervising. Empowerment without enablement is an insufficient strategy for helping teachers to become self-supervising.

There are situations, however, where teachers are not yet ready to be self-supervising. In those situations a skilled instructional supervisor collaborates with the teachers to help them recognize their professional needs, identify instructional problems to be solved, reach agreement on goals to improve instruction in their classrooms, and grow professionally.

Phase 2—Assessing Attitudes, Concepts, and Skills

Given the needs, problems, and improvement objectives identified by a self-supervising teacher or in collaboration with an instructional supervisor, the next phase focuses on assessing the teacher's attitudes toward the identified needs, problems, and objectives; assessing their level of mastery of the knowledge and skills required for effective performance; and setting goals to enhance their professional intellect.

Assessing the teacher's attitudes toward what they need to learn and how they need to learn it is the critical first step toward improved performance in the classroom. So, the early diagnostic activities focus on identifying the teacher's attitudes (which are mind-sets and can be positive, neutral, or negative). If the mind-sets are negative or neutral then a rationale for changing them is developed in collaboration with the teacher. If the mind-sets are positive then there is no need to change them.

When thinking about mind-set change, the first goal is not to force a person to change his or her mind about the problems that need to be solved or the goals that need to be achieved. Rather, the goal is to have the teacher become willing to consider with an open mind the changes that need to be made. Once they are willing to consider the changes then the second goal is to provide them with information and learning experiences that will convince them to change their minds.

After assessing attitudes, the teacher and supervisor collaborate to assess the teacher's professional concepts and skills using the mastery learning continuum (i.e., non-readiness, readiness, mastery, and maintenance).

Phase 3—Selecting or Designing Strategies for Change

After the Phase 2 assessment of attitudes, concepts, and skills are completed, the teacher then selects or designs strategies for improving his or her attitudes, concepts, and skills in ways that enhance his or her professional intellect and improve or maintain his or her teaching effectiveness. These strategies focus on changing attitudes about what they need to learn and on facilitating their learning of new knowledge and skills until they reach the level of maintenance on the mastery learning continuum.

The challenging process of changing attitudes (which are also known as mind-sets) needs a bit more explanation. To help teachers who have negative or neutral mind-sets toward desired changes a specially designed learning process needs to be used (see Duffy, 2009). The recommended process for expanding mind-sets has five steps:

Step 1: *Prepare*. Before providing any kind of training to introduce teachers to new knowledge and skills, the instructional supervisor must prepare to do that. Preparation includes developing a full understanding of what needs to be learned, how to learn it, and identifying the teachers' preferred learning styles (see Kolb, 1984, 1999) and information processing preferences (see Bandler & Grinder, 2005).

Step 2: *Educate*. Expanding mind-sets begins in conversations among colleagues in communities of practice (COPs) that are part of the KWS process. In these sessions, educators who understand the essential characteristics of the new knowledge and skills that teachers need to learn share their knowledge and open themselves to critical questions about the new knowledge and skills. The COPs are also provided with successful examples of how the new knowledge and skills have benefitted children, teachers, schools, and school systems.

Step 3: *Commit*. Once the teachers' mind-sets start to become open to considering new ways of doing things then it is time to start asking for their commitment to learn the new knowledge and skills. Their commitment will be demonstrated in their behavior as they solve problems, achieve goals, improve instruction, and enhance their professional intellect in ways that are strategically aligned with their cluster and district's transformation goals. As they implement their action plans, their observable behaviors will validate their commitment to the learning.

Step 4: *Tip*. As the teachers who started the diagnostic supervision process work through their commitment phase other teachers will be expected to join the process. At a point when approximately 25 percent (the critical mass needed to create change) of the teachers in a school system are using the new knowledge and skills required by the transformation, the system will reach a tipping point where the new knowledge and skills are rapidly disseminated throughout the entire system.

Step 5: *Shift*. When the tipping point is reached, there will be a sudden and dramatic shift that ensures that the changes created by the transformation process are embedded in the system and sustained for as long as they are producing desirable outcomes.

Enhancing Professional Intellect through Diagnostic Supervision

In chapter 2, I described several concepts, principles, and actions within the KWS methodology. One set of four actions was derived from the work of Pava (1983, pp. 92–110) where he discussed how to improve professional intellect and knowledge work. Those four actions adapted for school systems are as follows:

Step 5: Recycle to Pre-Launch Preparation   133

- Improve the quality and timeliness of information that teachers and support staff need to do their job effectively.
- Provide teachers and support staff with access to others who have the information they need.
- Provide teachers and support staff with many opportunities for exchanging information and knowledge with key others.
- Improve the quality and effectiveness of devices (equipment used to support teachers and support staff) and district-wide functions that are intended to support the core work processes (e.g., administration, curriculum development).

Diagnostic supervision is perfectly suited to adopt these actions to enhance the professional intellect of teachers and support staff.

INSTITUTIONALIZING IMPORTANT CHANGES

One of the big problems for all kinds of organizations, but especially for school systems, is the challenge of institutionalizing important changes (i.e., making sure changes stick). As many observers have noted, important changes are often swept out by new superintendents who want to make their own mark on their new school system. When the turnover rate among school superintendents is considered the failure to institutionalize important changes becomes painfully real.

Given the turnover rate in the superintendent's office, one institutionalization tactic is for a school board to create a policy that prevents new superintendents from stopping important and successful changes made by his or her predecessor that are still "in process" (i.e., not fully implemented). If the KWS On-Track Seminars provides data indicating that the changes being made through the transformation are effective even though they are not fully implemented then the school board policy should protect those effective changes by preventing the new superintendent from acting like the proverbial new broom that sweeps clean.

Institutionalization of change, which is an important goal of KWS Step 5, should not be confused with the practice of sustaining change. Sustainability can be viewed as preventing a school system from reverting to its "old ways" while the transformation process is in progress. Institutionalization focuses on keeping changes that are effective in place after the transformation is completed.

The Cornell HR Review (2013) identified several important actions for institutionalizing change. These actions include

- gaining high levels of commitment;
- reducing resistance;
- highlighting accomplishments;
- encouraging collaboration;
- training;
- communication; and
- appropriate incentive allocation to foster motivation.

Plans should be made during KWS Step 5 to engage in activities aligned with the above actions.

Monitoring Organization Culture

During KWS Step 5 it is also important for all change-leaders, especially the superintendent, to monitor their school system's culture to ensure that it is adaptive, dynamic, and open to change. A culture with these characteristics is absolutely critical for periodically recycling the KWS process to Step 1: Pre-Launch Preparation, thereby creating a transformation spiral that lifts the system upward toward higher and higher levels of performance.

Maintaining Strategic Alignment

In chapter 6, I presented information about creating strategic alignment. The alignment process ensures that the work of individuals is aligned with the goals of their teams, schools, and support work units; that the work of the teams, schools, and support work units is aligned with the goals of their clusters; and that the work of the clusters is aligned with the grand vision and strategic direction of the transformed school system. Everyone in a school district must be doing their part to help their district succeed within the context of the transformed system.

There are several tactics that can be used to maintain strategic alignment. They are briefly described below.

Use the Reward System

Thorndike (1898), a famous behavioral psychologist, identified what became known as the "Law of Effect." This law, in simple terms, states that behavior that is rewarded is repeated and behavior that is repeated is learned. Even though his theories of behavioral reinforcement are old, "Reinforcement is alive and strong as a concept in psychology" (Berridge, 2001, online document).

Although reinforcement theory has been demonstrated as a powerful way to influence human behavior, some people discount those theories and practices as manipulative. However, as Berridge noted, "The point is that all these processes of reward learning and motivation exist simultaneously as psychological processes. They are all within each of us, operating in parallel and usually in cooperation" (p. 277). Berridge also noted that "Reinforcement concepts still have detectable influence on research and theory today, in fields that range from behavioral neuroscience to human motivational psychology" (p. 271).

The big challenge with using reward systems to maintain strategic alignment is to ensure that the "right" behaviors are being rewarded. The right behaviors are those that unequivocally support the newly transformed school system's mission, vision, and strategic direction. Sometimes what happens is that the wrong behaviors are reinforced and then later repeated and learned. Here is a true story to sharpen that point.

Several years ago, I observed a young girl asking her mother for a soda. Mom said, "No." The girl started crying while continuing to ask for a soda. Mom said, "No." The girl cried louder while still asking for a soda. Mom said, "Okay, but just one."

I think it is easy to see that the wrong behavior was reinforced—the crying when told "no." I would predict that if crying was the girl's strategy for getting what she wanted, and if that was the mother's common response, then that crying behavior would be repeated and learned as a strategy for satisfying her "wants."

The lesson from the above anecdote is that change-leaders must ensure that rewards are given only to those who demonstrate behaviors that unequivocally support the transformed system's mission, vision, and strategic direction (Thorndike called those rewards "satisfiers"). There must also be well-defined consequences for not supporting the mission, vision, and strategic direction (Thorndike called consequences "annoyers"). The reward system is part of an organization's internal social infrastructure. That infrastructure is redesigned in KWS Step 2. The reward system must be redesigned early in the KWS Step 2 to comply with principles of behavioral reinforcement, recognition of accomplishments, ethics, fairness, and equity. The reward system should be redesigned to reward individual and team performance. A well-designed reward system can be a very powerful tool for creating and maintaining strategic alignment, for sustaining the transformation journey, and for institutionalizing effective changes after the journey is completed.

I also strongly recommend that authority to reward behavior that is unequivocally supporting the transformed system's mission, vision, and strategic direction should be pushed down to the level of the clusters within a school system. Each cluster should have the authority and resources to reward faculty and staff or to withhold rewards if their behavior is not supporting their cluster's efforts to support the district's performance. However, truly exceptional individual and team performance in support of the system's mission, vision, and strategic direction should be rewarded at the level of the whole system in district-wide ceremonies.

I once read about "critical lovers" versus "loving critics." I cannot remember or find the name of the person who coined those terms or where I first read about them. But I do remember that of the two, it is preferable to engage with loving critics. Think about a loving relationship you have or have had. How did it feel when that person was unlovingly critical of you or your ideas? Probably not good! Now, remember when you had a friend, spouse, life partner, or colleague who offered helpful criticism with love, kindness, and genuine concern for you; that is, they were loving critics. Much better feelings, right?

So, although I am a strong advocate for rewarding people for aligning themselves with their transformed school system's new mission, vision, and strategic direction, I am also a strong advocate for listening to those who perceive inefficiencies, injustices, and inequities in the design and functioning of the newly transformed system and who express their concerns out of genuine caring. Those loving critics should not be punished for voicing their concerns. Their concerns must be listened to, considered carefully, and then acted upon in the interest of creating a high-performing knowledge-creating school system. Don't punish the loving critics—welcome them and embrace their concerns.

Evaluating System Performance

There are many frameworks available for evaluating organization-wide performance. Deciding which framework to use depends on the design and purpose of the organization, the purpose of the evaluation, and the environment within which the organization exists. The evaluation framework chosen must ensure that the evaluation is done within the context of systems thinking; that is, the evaluation must consider how all the parts of the system are interconnected, how the parts are affected by other parts, and how high-performing parts of the system can be pressured by other low-performing parts into returning to an average-performing or low-performing status.

The evaluation framework I prefer is Stufflebeam's Context, Inputs, Processes, Product (CIPP) model for summative evaluation (2000) and Preskill and Torres's Evaluative Inquiry methodology for formative evaluation (1999). Both methods were described in chapter 9. Both models are theoretically and technically aligned with the notion that school districts are intact systems. Both are also systematic, meaning that they are structured in way that is organized and logically sequenced.

Evaluating Individual and Team Performance

As discussed in the previous chapter, I have mixed feelings about the traditional approaches to evaluating individual and team performance in school systems, especially in the era of standards, assessments, and accountability where test results are used to evaluate teachers and teams of teachers. I also have serious concerns about the ritualistic practice of observing classroom teaching for the purpose of evaluating a teacher's performance.

What bothers me about using test results to evaluate individual teachers and their teams is that I am not convinced that performance on a test is a valid indicator of what students learn and retain. Surely, you can easily recall studying for a test, taking the test, and then several days later forgetting what was covered on the test. Passing a test, in my opinion, is not an indicator of a student's learning; it is an indicator of a student's level of preparation for the test and a test of his or her memory.

Another issue sadly connected to using test results to evaluate individual and team performance is that the more important the test results are, the more likely it is that educators will "teach to the test." And, in worst case situations, educators will devise strategies for "massaging" the test results in their favor.

Traditional classroom observation also has its problems. A classroom observation is a snapshot, not a motion picture. The supervisor sees teaching behavior in a short period. He or she uses rubrics that supposedly represent effective teaching and uses some kind of data collection instrument or method. I don't care how well-constructed the rubrics are or how well-designed the data collection instrument or method is; it is impossible to control for the subjective biases of the observer.

Those subjective biases include the observer's preferred mental model for teaching (if the teacher's instructional methods do not conform to the observer's preferred mental model then the teacher might not be evaluated fairly or positively even if he or she is an excellent teacher); the observer's knowledge of what the teacher's pedagogical preferences look like (e.g., if the observer knows that the teacher is using a project-based learning method conjoined with the cooperative learning philosophy, if the observer is not intimately familiar with the principles and techniques supporting those methods then he or she cannot evaluate the teacher fairly or positively); the observer's capacity to record observable behavior, interpret that behavior in meaningful ways, and then organize the interpretations into useable feedback (in other words, the observer has to have a keen eye, an open mind, the ability to listen carefully, an intuitive sense to read between the lines of what is being observed, analytical abilities, and superior communication skills); and, finally, the observer's relationship with the person being observed (i.e., if the supervisor has a friendly relationship with the teacher being observed then that relationship would likely have a positive effect on the evaluation while if the relationship was strained then that would likely have a negative effect on the evaluation).

Given my concerns about evaluating individual and team performance, I fully understand that it is important to ensure that the work of teachers and their teams are aligned with their transformed system's new mission, vision, and strategic direction.

How to do this will vary from school district to school district, but however it is done it must be done in ways that collect valid and reliable data about individual and team performance and must be fair and equitable.

Strategic Communication

Another process during KWS Step 5 is strategic communication (Duffy & Chance, 2006). Strategic communication is an extraordinarily important process that focuses on influencing stakeholder behavior to gain and maintain support for a school system's posttransformation performance. Frequently, this process is managed by a school system's public relations staff. Definitely much more than a set of tools, strategic communication is a process in which answers are sought for what can be misleadingly simple questions such as:

- Who do we need to talk to? (the audience)
- What do they want to hear? (the message)
- Why do we want to communicate with the audience? (the goals)
- How do we communicate? (the tactics)

The strategic communication process has four phases: structuring information, preparing content, delivering the content, and persisting in delivering a consistent message to all audiences. Each phase is briefly described below.

Structuring Information

This activity focuses on collecting data about the benefits of the changes that were made and the costs associated with creating those benefits (i.e., a cost-benefit analysis). The data are then organized into information that is structured to fit with the characteristics of the audience for whom it is intended.

Preparing Content

Next, the school system's public relations staff prepare several different messages, each one designed with the intended audience in mind. Although each message is designed differently, the core message should be the same; that is,

"We transformed our system and we created significant changes to benefit our students, our faculty and staff, and our community."

Delivering the Content

This is the phase were the messages are delivered to the intended audiences. The messages should be delivered in ways that fit with the audience; for example, using online communication (Facebook, Twitter), written communication (letters sent to key stakeholders), and special presentations (large group meetings supported by PowerPoint slides).

Persisting in Delivering Consistent Messages

When delivering messages it is important not to assume that the messages are heard or understood the first time they are communicated. People are notorious for not "hearing" the message the first time it is delivered. Therefore, it is very important to repeat the messages several times using several different media.

CONCLUSION

The length of time needed to transform a school system can range from eighteen to thirty-six months for small- to medium-sized systems and five–seven years for larger systems. Transformation is also costly in terms of the financial, technical, and human resources that are invested in the process. Given the time and the costs, it is imperative that change-leaders continue to evaluate and monitor their transformed school systems' performance from the time the transformation is completed until the time they are ready to launch another round of transformation. If KWS Step 5 is ignored or if it is not implemented with due diligence, it is possible that all of the good changes that were made will disappear thereby creating significant resistance to future calls for change—resistance that will probably be impossible to overcome.

REFERENCES

Bandler, R. and Grinder, J. (2005). *The structure of magic (Vol. 1): A book about language and therapy* (1st ed.). Palo Alto, CA: Science and Behavior Books.

Berridge, K. C. (2001). Reward learning: Reinforcement, incentives, and expectations *The Psychology of Learning and Motivation, 40*, 223–278. Available from: http://lsa.umich.edu/psych/research&labs/berridge/publications/Berridge2001Rewardlearningchapter.pdf.

Chassin, M. R. and O'Kane, M. E. (online, date unknown). History of the Quality Improvement Movement. Retrieved on February 15, 2016, from: http://www2.aap.org/sections/perinatal/pdf/1quality.pdf.

Cogan, M. (1972). *Clinical supervision.* Boston, MA: Houghton Mifflin.

Cornell HR Review (2013, October 14). Change management and organizational effectiveness for the HR professional. Retrieved on February 15, 2016, from: http://www.cornellhrreview.org/change-management-and-organizational-effectiveness-for-the-hr-professional/.

Duffy, F. M. (2009). Paradigms, mental models, and mindsets: Triple barriers to transformational change in school systems. Available from: http://cnx.org/content/col10723/latest/.

Duffy, F. M. & Chance, P. L. (2006). *Strategic communication during whole-system change: Advice and guidance for school district leaders and PR specialists.* Leading Systemic School Improvement Series. Lanham, MD: Rowman & Littlefield Education.

Kolb, D. (1984). *Experiential learning: experience as the source of learning and development.* Englewood Cliffs, NJ: Prentice Hall.

Kolb D. (1999). *The Kolb learning style inventory (version 3).* Boston, MA: Hay Group.

Lapcevic, P. S. (1974). *The application of experiences in two in-service programs to the development of a paradigm for diagnostic supervision.* (Unpublished doctoral dissertation, University of Pittsburgh, 1974). *Dissertation Abstracts International*, 35/01, 171A. University Microfilms No. 74-15, 629.

Minnesota Office of Continuous Improvement (online, date unknown). CI Resource Library. Retrieved on February 15, 2016, from: http://mn.gov/admin/lean/resources/ci-tools/.

Pasmore, W. A. (1988). *Designing effective organizations: The sociotechnical systems perspective.* New York: Wiley & Sons.

Pasmore, W. A. (1992). *Sociotechnical systems design for total quality.* San Francisco, CA: Organizational Consultants.

Pava, C. H. P. (1983, Spring). Designing managerial and professional work for high performance: A sociotechnical approach. *National Productivity Review, 2*(2), 126–135. DOI: 10.1002/npr.4040020204.

Preskill, H. and Torres, R. T. (1999). *Evaluative inquiry for learning in organizations.* Thousand Oaks, CA: Sage.

Seager, G. B., Jr. (1971). Evaluation of a diagnostic instrument of supervision. University of Pittsburgh. ERIC Number ED052222. Available from: http://files.eric.ed.gov/fulltext/ED052222.pdf.

Seager, G. B. (1974). An introduction to diagnostic supervision. Unpublished paper, University of Pittsburgh.

Stufflebeam, D. L. (2000). The CIPP model for evaluation. In D. L. Stufflebeam, G. F. Madaus, and T. Kellaghan (Eds.). Evaluation models: Viewpoints on educational and human services evaluation. Boston: Kluwer Academic (pp. 279–317).

Thorndike, E. L. (1898). *Animal intelligence: An experimental study of the associative processes in animals.* New York: Macmillan.

Section 3

PREPARING KNOWLEDGE WORK SUPERVISORS

Transforming an entire school system using Knowledge Work Supervision is a complex challenge. Complex, however, doesn't mean impossible—it means there is a lot to do and it has to be done correctly. Because of this requirement it is imperative that a new professional role be created called "Knowledge Work Supervisor." Chapter 9 offers a design for a Change-Leadership Academy that would provide training to educators seeking the role of Knowledge Work Supervisor. Finally, chapter 10 presents a rationale for revolutionary change in our education system and its component school districts.

Chapter Nine

Preparing Knowledge Work Supervisors

DESIGNING A CHANGE-LEADERSHIP ACADEMY

Formal programs to prepare Knowledge Work Supervisors are needed if school systems are to be transformed to conform to the requirements of our twenty-first-century knowledge-age society. In this chapter, I offer a design for a "Change-Leadership Academy" that can be situated in university-based education leadership programs or offered by a consortium of school systems that are geographically close to each other. This academy will train teams of change-leaders from school systems to use Knowledge Work Supervision (KWS) to transform:

1. their district's relationship with its external environment;
2. teaching and learning to provide all students with a customized, personalized learning experience;
3. the work processes required to support effective teaching and learning; and
4. their district's internal social infrastructure.

There is an extraordinary need in the field of education to transform entire school systems to provide children with an education that will help them succeed in America's twenty-first-century society. This need has been referred to and documented throughout this book. There is also much advice and guidance in the field of education about *why* transformational change is needed. There is a lot of information about *what* the outcomes of transformational change should be. But, there is very little information about *how* to create and sustain whole-system transformational change. This book and the proposed Change-Leadership Academy focuses on the "how."

Some of the "how" advice found in the literature focuses on training educators how to replicate the successful transformations of the selected school systems. However, experience shows that attempting to replicate the successful transformation of other school systems is a low-success strategy. For example, Roger Sampson, the superintendent who led the Chugach district in Alaska to its Baldrige Quality Award and the former president of the Education Commission of the States, cofounded the Reinventing Schools Coalition (RISC) to train educators about how to replicate the Chugach experience. According to Sampson, of twenty-plus systems receiving training on how to replicate the Chugach experience, only three were successful. *The proposed Change-Leadership Academy does not train educators how to replicate the successes of other school systems. Rather, it teaches them core concepts, principles, and skills that will help them transform their systems in accordance with their vision for the future of their systems.*

Research on and experience with transformational change suggests that the best way to transform any system is for that system to use a methodology and tools that help people in those systems to create and sustain transformational change that is tailored to their unique system characteristics. *The proposed Change-Leadership Academy will do this.*

Yet, despite what we know about creating and sustaining transformational change, there seems to be no formal, sustained skill-based program that trains teams of educators to create and sustain transformational change and, at the same time, provides them with technical assistance and coaching to implement what they learn in the training event. *The proposed Change-Leadership Academy is a sustained skill-based program that also provides technical assistance and coaching services.*

Further, research on the transfer of learning (Gardner & Korth, 1997) suggests that learning that occurs in a training program is more effective if teams participate in the training. *The proposed Change-Leadership Academy is team-based. Also, an academy community of practice (COP) is formed comprised of change-leadership teams from across the United States and the world who currently enrolled in the academy or who have completed the academy training.*

Degree programs focusing on education leadership are inappropriate for training teams of educators about how to create and sustain transformational change. The proposed Change-Leadership Academy is not a degree-granting program. It is, instead, a professional development opportunity offering continuing education credits for teams of educators from school systems throughout the United States. *However, even though the proposed Change-Leadership Academy would not lead to a degree, it could be situated within degree-granting university-based education leadership programs; alternatively, it could be offered by state departments of education as a continuing education program whereby participants would earn continuing education credits.*

The Change-Leadership Academy's Mission

The Change-Leadership Academy trains teams of educators from carefully selected school systems about how to transform their school systems by making simultaneous changes along three change paths: Path 1, transform the relationship their districts have with their external environments; Path 2, transform teaching and learning to provide students with a personalized learning experience; and Path 3, transform the internal social infrastructure of their districts.

The Vision for the Change-Leadership Academy Experience

Visualize community leaders, parents, students, and teachers working together in a large-group framing and defining their dreams, aspirations, and strategic goals for their school systems. See all these participants energized by their productive collaboration and developing feelings of ownership for the dreams, aspirations, and goals. Where there is a need, envision participants becoming inspired to fill that need. Where there is an opportunity, see others defining the goals for and the potential of those opportunities

Imagine the excitement in the air as district-level administrators, principals, teachers, and support personnel use the outcomes of the earlier community gathering to redesign their systems. Feel the palpable energy of system transformation fueled by grassroots involvement, unleashed creativity, and, most of all, commitment from all the key players that make a system perform. Taste the sweetness of success as dreams, aspirations, and goals are realized as never before.

Sense the power of a school system where teachers come together often in COPs to create more effective strategies for teaching and learning; where teachers, parents, and administrators collaborate on teams to find creative solutions to help students become more proficient in their learning; and where students pool their learning to present knowledgeable presentations and documents on various topics.

Imagine a school system that cares as much for the adults who work in the system as it does for the students. See these professionals creating opportunities for teachers and professional staff to enhance their professional intellect.

Observe a school system not engaged in yearly rapid-fire change, yet having the capacity to sustain change over time. See that system harnessing the collective power of its human, technical, financial, and time resources and focusing them on creating and sustaining a high performing school system.

Note that this is a vision for school systems transformed under the leadership of Knowledge Work Supervisors trained by the Change-Leadership Academy.

A PROPOSED DESIGN FOR THE CHANGE-LEADERSHIP ACADEMY

The Change-Leadership Academy trains teams of change-leaders from carefully selected school systems to use the KWS methodology and tools to transform:

1. a district's relationship with its external environment;
2. teaching and learning to provide all students with a customized, personalized learning experience;
3. the work processes needed to support effective teaching and learning; and
4. their district's internal social infrastructure.

The academy experience begins with a one-week, in-residence summer training event. During that first week of training, the teams learn core concepts for mastering the art and science of transforming school systems. The product for the first week of training is an action plan to engage faculty and staff in the participants' school systems in KWS Step 1.

At the conclusion of the summer training, participating teams return to their school systems to engage in a year-long "Preparing for Transformational Change Seminar" that helps the participating teams to implement KWS Step 1 (the preparation activities are taught to the teams during their first week of summer training). The products for the *Preparing for Transformational Change Seminar* are:

1. a team learning plan to help members become masters of the art and science of transforming school systems;
2. a comprehensive action plan to prepare their school systems to engage in transformational change; and
3. a five-day training design to teach their colleagues about core concepts and principles of transformational change.

During the year-long seminar, KWS experts will be available to the teams to provide technical assistance and coaching. Participants are linked to a COP comprised of academy participants throughout the United States and the world. This COP provides academy participants with the opportunity to communicate with each other online about what they are doing, what they are learning, obstacles they are facing, their solutions for overcoming the obstacles, and so on.

The participating teams return to the Change-Leadership Academy for a second week-long summer of training event. During the second week, they learn additional ideas and tools for implementing and facilitating KWS. An important activity during the second week asks participating teams to share their comprehensive action plans and five-day training institute designs with their Change-Leadership Academy peers so they can receive feedback about the strengths and weaknesses of their plans.

Following the second summer of change-leadership training, the participating teams are expected to implement their plans to transform their school systems using the KWS methodology. KWS experts will be available to those teams to provide fee-based technical assistance and coaching until the systems are transformed.

A logic model illustrating the conceptual design of the academy is displayed in figure 9.1.

THE TRAINING CURRICULUM

A proposed training curriculum for the Change Leadership Academy is presented below.

Learning Outcomes for the Change-Leadership Academy Experience

Participants in the Change-Leadership Academy will benefit from the following learning outcomes (LOs):

- LO 1.0: Recognize the challenges facing America's school system.
- LO 2.0: Recognize the needs and opportunities that those challenges represent for their school systems.
- LO 3.0: Recognize the limitations of the Industrial-Age paradigm for teaching and learning and understand the promise of the Knowledge-Age paradigm (i.e., learner-centered teaching and learning).
- LO 4.0: Understand core concepts and principles of transformational change.
- LO 5.0: Understand the KWS methodology for creating and sustaining transformational change.
- LO 6.0: Design a personal learning plan to become masters of the art and science of transforming school systems.
- LO 7.0: Create and implement a comprehensive action plan to transform their school systems.
- LO 8.0: Design a five-day training institute to teach their colleagues about core concepts and principles of transformational change.

Situation	Inputs	Outputs		Outcomes		
		Activities	Participants	Short-Term	Mid-Term	Long-Term
		What We Do	**Who We Reach**	**Short-Term Results**	**Mid-Term Results**	**Long-Term Results**
Failure of the industrial-age model of education.	**What We Invest**	Identify, screen and select teams of change leaders from school systems that desire to transform.	Carefully selected school systems that desire to engage in transformational change.	A maximum of four school systems participate in the Academy every year.	The change leadership teams initiate KWS Step 1: Pre-Launch Preparation during the training program.	Transformed school systems
Children left behind	Expertise					No children left behind.
Bureaucratic organization design	Financial, technical, and human resources		The students in those school systems.	Teams learn principles of transformational change and a transformational change methodology.	Participating school systems achieve a level of readiness and develop the capacity to continue their transformation journey.	Children prepared for success in our 21st century society.
Inattention to the quality of worklife for teachers and support staff	High quality training design and delivery system	Design and offer training and technical assistance to help participating teams to create and sustain transformational change.	Faculty and staff in the school systems.			Enhanced teacher and support staff motivation, job satisfaction, and effectiveness
Inattention to relationships with the external environment	Access to national-level experts		The communities within which the school systems exist.			
Three change paths to transform school system; not just one.	Coaching and technical assistance					

				External Environment		
	Assumptions					
Focus of Evaluation	Collect Data	Formative and Summative Evaluation Analyze and Interpret Data			Report Results	

Figure 9.1 Logic Model for the Proposed Change Leadership Academy

FINAL THOUGHTS AND RECOMMENDATIONS

I strongly recommend that state departments of education create a professional certificate or license for Knowledge Work Supervisors (see Appendix A that presents a set of research-based standards for preparing Knowledge Work Supervisors and Appendix B that presents proposed requirements for creating a state department of education professional certificate for Knowledge Work Supervisors). By doing this, the state departments of education will be communicating the value they place on this new leadership position. Further, if the state departments of education create a professional certification for Knowledge Work Supervisors then university-based education leadership programs and education administration programs will respond by creating degree-granting change-leadership programs that would include the same content that is embedded in the Change-Leadership Academy.

REFERENCES

Gardner, B. S. and Korth, S.J. (1997). Classroom strategies that facilitate transfer of learning to the workplace. *Innovative Higher Education, 22*(1). Available from: http://www2.sfasu.edu/cte/Michelle_Files/HMS_300_Web_Content/Classroom_Strat.pdf.

Chapter Ten

Prologue to Revolution

> Though we often prefer to believe that nothing can be done about the ... problems we face, there comes a time when we have to take on the system because the system needs to change. There comes a time when we need to "just do it."
>
> —R. E. Quinn, *Deep Change: Discovering the Leader Within* (1996)

The historical chronicles of the world are replete with examples of episodic revolutions. One of those revolutions was enacted by arms-bearing revolutionaries seeking freedom from tyranny (the American Revolution, 1776). Other revolutions in history were driven by frame-breaking innovative ideas and technologies (e.g., airplane flight, computers, and the Internet). Even the field of education experienced a revolution in the eighteenth century when the Agrarian Age paradigm for educating children shifted to the Industrial Age paradigm, a paradigm that still controls the design, performance, and outcomes of school systems.

The societies of most modernized countries and their organizations and institutions have moved far into a new societal era—an era commonly referred to as the Information Age, the Knowledge Age, or the Conceptual Age. The name of this era notwithstanding, one thing is clear: this era is significantly, substantively, and qualitatively different from the Industrial Age.

Because the requirements for success in the Knowledge Age are so different from the requirements for success in the Industrial Age, our children deserve and need an education that prepares them to succeed in this new age. An education cast in the mold of the Industrial Age cannot and will not help our children succeed in our twenty-first-century society. An education cast in the mold of the Industrial Age does and always will leave children behind. The systems, in other words, are perfectly designed to get the results they are getting.

DRIVING OUT FOUR INDUSTRIAL AGE PARADIGMS

Providing our children with an education that satisfies the requirements of our twenty-first-century Knowledge Age requires a paradigm-shifting revolution that drives out four old interconnected Industrial Age paradigms that influence the design and performance of our education systems and their component school systems. The four paradigm shifts are described below:

Paradigm Shift 1: Transform the way school systems interact with external stakeholders (move from a crisis-oriented, reactive approach to an opportunity-seeking, proactive approach).

Paradigm Shift 2: Transform the way teachers teach and how children learn (shift from group-based, teacher-centered instruction to personalized learner-centered instruction) and the way academic and nonacademic support services are designed, managed, and delivered (redesign them to ensure that these services are aligned with the requirements of personalized learning).

Paradigm Shift 3: Transform the design of the internal social infrastructure of school systems (shift from a mechanistic, bureaucratic organization design to an organic, participative design) and the organization culture, the reward system, the job descriptions, and so on (align them with the requirements of the new core and support work processes).

Paradigm Shift 4: Transform the way in which educators create change (shift from piecemeal change strategies to whole-system change strategies).

Further, there are several reasons why a revolution in thinking, believing, and working in school systems is needed (rather than relying on evolution or depending on the continuous improvement of the status quo):

- The existing four paradigms that control the field of education are hammered in hard and are extraordinarily resistant to change.
- The existing four paradigms are locked in place by popular mental models, change-resistant mindsets, and careers and reputations built on the old paradigms and mental models.
- The existing four paradigms are protected by institutionalized policies, procedures, laws, reward systems, tradition, the organization design of school systems, and the organization culture.

If our children are to receive the education they deserve and need to succeed in our twenty-first-century society, then the four old paradigms need to be driven out, not tweaked, not continuously improved, and not fixed piecemeal. Driving out these old paradigms requires a revolution and revolution-minded change-leaders.

REVOLUTION REQUIRES POLITICAL ADVOCACY, COURAGE, PASSION, AND VISION

Although a revolution to drive out the old paradigms requires muscular political advocacy, if you step forward to lead or join this revolution on the front lines of change, you will require much more than just political advocacy. Fighting this revolution requires significant courage, passion, and vision. You must have courage to stand and fight for what you believe in. You need passion to give you the emotional energy and resilience you need to persevere. And, you must have a vision to serve as your North Star to keep moving in the right direction. Further, these three traits—courage, passion, and vision—must be simultaneously present in each change-leader. A change-leader may have courage but lack passion and vision. A change-leader may have a powerful vision but lack the courage to fight for it. A change-leader may have courage and a vision but lack the passion to pursue the vision relentlessly. All three traits must be present all at once in each man and woman who steps forward to lead this revolution.

The Past Before Us Is Not the Future

Our societies cannot afford to carry their old education paradigms forward. It does no good to dream of an idealized future for education if that future is just a projection and continuation of the past. Instead, change-minded revolutionaries should imagine that the four paradigms controlling the design and performance of the education system and its component school systems were destroyed last night and now they must invent four new paradigms. The main features of these new paradigms have been highlighted above.

For years, progressive thinkers throughout the world have called for systemic transformational change in school systems. And for the same amount of time, the four dominant paradigms have not yielded their control of education. I think there are at least five reasons for this stubborn resistance to change:

1. Some educators, consultants, and policymakers do not understand the meaning of systemic transformational change.
2. Some educators, consultants, and policymakers have a difficult time "seeing" school districts as intact systems; instead, they view them as a confederation of loosely coupled schools.
3. Those educators, consultants, and policymakers who do understand the meaning of systemic transformational change and who do see school districts as intact, organic, adaptive systems are uncomfortable with the complexity and messiness of transformational change.

4. Those educators, consultants, and policymakers who do understand the meaning of systemic transformational change and who do see school districts as intact, organic, adaptive systems are uncomfortable with the amount of time it takes to create and sustain transformational change.
5. Those educators, consultants, and policymakers who do understand the meaning of systemic transformational change and who do see school districts as intact, organic, adaptive systems do not know how to create and sustain transformational change, so they avoid doing it.

Given the above five reasons for resisting transformational change, creating and sustaining a revolution to drive out the four controlling paradigms will require change-leaders who are masters of transformational change (Duffy, 2010). Masters of transformational change influence the design, performance, and outcomes of their school systems by making innovative, but feasible, choices about how to teach children, about how children learn, about how to treat the professionals who work in their systems, about how their systems interact with the external environment, and about how to create and sustain transformational change. Masters of transformation possess knowledge, skills, and dispositions that are organized into three broad competency sets:

- Mastery of Awareness—paying attention to opportunities and threats in the external environment; identifying promising trends; anticipating political support or opposition; recognizing demographic changes in the community.
- Mastery of Deliberate Intention—envisioning a promising future for the school system; focusing on the vision and creating strategic, tactical, and operational plans to achieve the vision; rewarding people for working in support of the vision.
- Mastery of Methodology—adopting a methodology designed to transform school systems; developing skills for using the methodology, its core concepts and principles, and its tools (see volume 2 of this set for guidance on training to become masters of the Knowledge Work Supervision methodology).

A CALL TO ACTION: JOIN THE REVOLUTION TO TRANSFORM AMERICA'S SCHOOL SYSTEMS

The education revolutionaries in our country have already made a decision to promote paradigm change in school systems. As people who may be considering joining this revolution, I want to ask you five questions. Please consider your answers carefully and please answer them with an unqualified "yes" or "no." If you feel a need to qualify your answer, then that qualification is considered a "no."

1. Do you believe that our society has evolved into the Knowledge Age?
2. Do you believe that the field of education has not coevolved with our society?
3. Do you believe that entire school systems need to be transformed if we want the field of education to align with the requirements of the Knowledge Age?
4. Do you believe that school-aged children (present and future) deserve an education that prepares them for success in our Knowledge Age societies?
5. Do you believe that it is unethical, and perhaps immoral, for school systems to leave some children behind as they participate in the systems' teaching and learning processes?

If you answered "yes" to all of these questions, then I have two more questions to ask you:

1. Given your answers, what are you going to do about it?
2. When will you start?

Before you take action, please be warned that you should not accept lightly this call to action. Leading or participating in a revolution against the four dominant paradigms controlling the field of education will require substantial courage, passion, and vision because you may be scorned, you may be ostracized, you may be ridiculed, and you may be punished for your heresy. If you are unwilling to endure these consequences, or if you do not have the emotional and physical stamina to persevere and help achieve the strategic goals of the revolution, then please consider other ways of helping.

But ... if you do have courage, passion, and vision to endure the consequences of rebellion, and if you answered "yes" to all of the first five questions, those of us who are advocates of a revolution to displace the four old paradigms need your help. We need you to join with us to drive out the old paradigms.

Here's what you can do—right now—to become a part of this revolution. Think of one person—just one—who you believe shares your dream for transforming your school system for success in the twenty-first century. Call or e-mail that person and make an appointment to visit with him or her for 30 minutes or less. During the meeting, share highlights from what you learned in this prologue and talk about the people and organizations you found in this directory. Communicate the need to transform your school system. Ask for his or her support to help build a coalition for change. Then, do it! Make it happen! Start to prepare your system for a journey unlike any other it has experienced in the past—start dreaming, creating, and sustaining transformational change built on the principles of the four new paradigms discussed in this prologue.

Once you have a powerful and committed coalition in place, start moving toward an idealized design for your school system that educates students by providing them with a personalized, customized, learner-centered education experience; that provides the faculty and staff in your districts with a satisfying and motivating work life; that helps your district create and sustain proactive, opportunity-seeking relationships with its external environment; and that introduces into your district a methodology for creating and sustaining whole-system change.

If you are already engaging in a revolution to drive out the four dominant Industrial Age paradigms that influence the design and performance of school systems, or if you are intending to join the revolution, then I also encourage you to consider collaborating with other revolutionaries so we can coordinate our efforts to create effective strategies and tactics for transforming education systems and their component school systems.

The suggestion to collaborate, however, also represents a difficult challenge because some of the revolutionaries in the field of education today want *their* ideas, *their* models, and *their* methodologies to win the day and bring them fame. This desire for ego gratification creates situations where those motivated by this egocentric need do not want to collaborate with others and also do not consider with care the ideas of others. The need for a coordinated effort to transform school systems, however, is so important that we cannot afford to work as if our ideas were the only ones that mattered. We must look for a way to consolidate our ideas, to create a unified strategic framework for transforming school systems, and to build a powerful political and grassroots coalition to support systemic transformational change.

By taking the above three actions (talking with a colleague, starting to transform your district, and affiliating with other revolutionaries), you will be joining with colleagues who are striving to drive out the old paradigms influencing the design and performance of school systems throughout the world to create and sustain new school systems designed to align with the four new Knowledge Age paradigms. Can you think of a more important dream to turn into reality for our children, grandchildren, and generations of children yet unborn?

A PARTING REFLECTION

Finally, I leave you with a parting reflection from a book by Olive Schreiner (1998, originally published in 1883), a South African peace and antiapartheid campaigner. In her book *The Story of a South African Farm*, there is an allegory about "The Hunter." He has been hunting for the white bird of truth for his entire life. As part of his search, he built a stone staircase into the sky.

There is a point in the story where he is about ready to give up his search because of fatigue from the hunting and building, and he says

> My strength is gone. When I lie down worn out, others will stand young and fresh. By the stairs I have built, they will mount. They will never know the name of the person who made them. At the clumsy work they will laugh, when the stones roll, they will curse me. But they will mount, and on my work, they will climb, and by my stair.

That staircase was the Hunter's legacy for future generations. What will your legacy be as a change-leader who envisions transformational change in your school system? What will your "staircase" be? If you choose to dream, create, and sustain transformational change, if you are willing and able to join the needed revolution, then you must do so with courage, passion, and vision. Build that stair toward a desirable future for your school systems. And, keep hope alive!

REFERENCES

Duffy, F. M. (2010). *Dream! Create! Sustain!: Mastering the art and science of transforming school systems.* Leading Systemic School Improvement Series. Lanham, MD: Rowman & Littlefield Education.

Quinn, R. E. (1996). *Deep change: Discovering the leader within.* Jossey-Bass Business and Management Series. San Francisco: Jossey-Bass.

Schreiner, O. (1998, original work published 1883). The hunter's allegory. *The story of a South African farm.* Mineola, NY: Dover.

Appendices

Appendix A. National Framework of Professional Standards for Change-Leadership in Education (Duffy, 2010)

Performance Standards, Criteria, and Rubrics for Graduate-Level Change-Leadership in Education Programs

Standards of Performance	Sample Knowledge, Skills, and Dispositions for Each Standard
Standard 1.0—Systems Thinking: A change leader perceives school districts as intact, organic systems and explains how districts function as systems.	*Knowledge* explains in detail the key features of school district as a system. *Skill* analyzes in detail the functional properties of school districts as systems. *Disposition* fully accepts the school districts intact, organic systems.
Standard 2.0—Focus of Systemic Transformational Change: A change leader understands that transforming an entire school district requires improvements in student, faculty and staff, and whole-system learning.	*Knowledge* describes the importance of whole-system improvement in rich detail. *Skill* collects and interprets data about the need for change. *Disposition* accepts the importance of whole-district learning and can explain that importance in rich detail.
Standard 3.0—Initiating Change: A change leader creates the case for systemic transformation within school districts and in communities by providing data to support both the *need* for change and the *opportunities* that can be seized by engaging in change.	*Knowledge* explains in rich detail a strong rationale for creating and sustaining whole-district change. *Skill* uses tools and processes for gaining and sustaining internal and external political support for change. *Disposition* enthusiastically endorses the concept of whole-system change.

(continued)

Appendix A (continued)

Standards of Performance	Sample Knowledge, Skills, and Dispositions for Each Standard
Standard 4.0—Assessing the Impact of Change: A change leader assesses the breadth, depth, sustainability and anticipated positive outcomes of a systemic transformational change strategy.	*Knowledge* explains in rich detail the breadth, depth, sustainability, and expected returns from engaging in whole-system change. *Skill* conducts an in-depth analysis of the breadth, depth, sustainability, and expected returns from engaging in whole-system change. *Disposition* accepts the fact that whole-system change is complex and requires careful planning and acts on this acceptance.
Standard 5.0—Facilitating Change: A change leader helps colleagues and community members gain insight into the human dynamics of system transformation and develops their confidence to achieve transformation goals.	*Knowledge* possesses advanced level of knowledge of facilitation skills. *Skill* facilitates interpersonal and group behavior effectively. *Disposition* is a strong advocate for helping people understand the nature of change prior to launching a change effort.
Standard 6.0: Developing Political Support for Change: A change leader develops political support for systemic transformation through effective change-leadership.	*Knowledge* explains in rich detail strategies and tactics for building political support. *Skill* demonstrates sophisticated skills for developing political support. *Disposition* is a staunch advocate for acting in a political way to gain political support for change.
Standard 7.0—Expanding Mindsets: A change leader engages in and shares with colleagues personal learning to deepen and broaden personal mindsets about why systemic transformation of school districts is necessary and about the best strategy for creating and sustaining transformational change.	*Knowledge* provides a detailed and cogent rationale for engaging in personal learning. *Skill* develops a detailed and feasible plan to engage in personal learning. *Disposition* is a strong advocate for engaging in personal learning.
Standard 8.0—Planning Systemic Transformational Change: A change leader formulates and leads the implementation of a plan to create and sustain systemic transformation in school districts.	*Knowledge* understands the complexity of planning for change and describes the key elements of change plans. *Skill* demonstrates advanced skills for planning for system-wide change. *Disposition* is a powerful advocate for engaging in good planning for change.

Appendix A (continued)

Standards of Performance	Sample Knowledge, Skills, and Dispositions for Each Standard
Standard 9.0: Demonstrating Disposition for Change-Leadership: A change leader demonstrates high personal commitment to achieving transformation goals through courage, passion, and vision while striving to remain calm in the chaos of system-wide transformation.	*Knowledge* provides a powerful rationale for leading change with courage, passion, and vision while remaining calm. *Skill* demonstrates advanced skills for managing personal calmness during change. *Disposition* is a strong advocate for the importance of leading change with courage, passion, and vision.
Standard 10.0—Mastering the Art and Science of Systemic Transformational Change: A change leader is familiar with and skillful in using a variety of change theories, tools, and methodologies derived from interdisciplinary perspectives on change leadership and systemic transformation.	*Knowledge* explains in great detail at least one methodology for creating and sustaining whole-system change; including tools and processes that are part of that methodology. *Skill* applies at least one methodology for creating and sustaining whole-system change; including tools and processes that are part of that methodology. *Disposition* is a vocal advocate for the importance of change leaders knowing, understanding, and applying change theories and tools.

*Duffy, F. M. (2010). Dream! create! sustain!: Mastering the art & science of transforming school systems. Leading Systemic School Improvement Series. Lanham, MD: Rowman & Littlefield Education.

Appendix B. Proposed Certification Requirements for Knowledge Work Supervisors

Role Description	The Knowledge Work Supervisor role is essential for effective transformation. This role provides tactical leadership by coordinating on a daily basis the work of several change-leadership teams.
	The Knowledge Work Supervisor is also responsible for developing communication links between and among the district's various subsystems and between the district and its external stakeholders. Communication is also critical for managing the change process within the school system.
Personality Traits and Learning Style	Because of the nature of this role, it is absolutely critical that this person has the following core personality and learning-style traits: the conceptual ability of a systems-thinker; extraordinary interpersonal and group communication skills;

(continued)

Appendix B (*continued*)

Personality Traits and Learning Style	the conceptual ability of an innovative-thinker; an understanding of how to use information technology to create and spread professional knowledge within school systems; tolerance of ambiguity; and willingness to take risks.
Education Requirements	A graduate degree in education leadership from an accredited university and successful completion of a Change-Leadership Academy that provided training in the following areas (see Appendix A): Systems thinking (Standard 1). Systemic transformational change (Standard 2). Initiating change (Standard 3). Assessing the impact of change (Standard 4). Facilitating change (Standard 5). Developing political support for change (Standard 6). Expanding mind-sets (Standard 7). Planning systemic transformational change (Standard 8). Demonstrating a disposition for change leadership (Standard 9). Mastering the art and science of transformational change (Standard 10).
Experience Requirements	Three to five years of proven and successful formal or informal leadership experience in school systems. Documented experience as an innovator. Documented successful experience as an effective member of teams. Documented successful experience facilitating groups of professionals in creative problem-solving situations Documented knowledge and skills in the seven areas listed above under "education requirements." Documented success as a creator of change.